METAPHILOSOPHY AND FREE WILL

METAPHILOSOPHY
AND FREE WILL

Richard Double

New York   Oxford
OXFORD UNIVERSITY PRESS
1996

Oxford University Press

Oxford New York
Athens   Auckland   Bangkok   Bogota   Bombay
Buenos Aires   Calcutta   Cape Town   Dar es Salaam
Delhi   Florence   Hong Kong   Istanbul   Karachi
Kuala Lumpur   Madras   Madrid   Melbourne
Mexico City   Nairobi   Paris   Singapore
Taipei   Tokyo   Toronto

and associated companies in
Berlin   Ibadan

Published by Oxford University Press, Inc.
198 Madison Avenue, New York, New York 10016

Oxford is a registered trademark of Oxford University Press

Library of Congress Cataloging-in-Publication Data
Double, Richard.
Metaphilosophy and free will / Richard Double.
   p.   cm.
Includes bibliographical references and index.
ISBN 0-19-510762-4
1. Free will and determinism.   2. Methodology.   I. Title.
BJ1468.5.D68   1996
123'.5—dc20   95-50082

9 8 7 6 5 4 3 2 1

Printed in the United States of America
on acid-free paper

FOR
LORI MONIQUE EASON
WITH LOVE

Acknowledgments

Many persons contributed to this book. Three excellent analytical philosophers—Mark Bernstein, Alfred Mele, and Bruce Waller—provided meticulous, invaluable commentary on the entire manuscript. Others helped with chapters and papers that went into chapters: my Edinboro University colleagues Edmund Abegg, Dana Bushnell, and Robert Cogan; Jonathan Bennett, Richard Brook, David Cockburn, Tomis Kapitan, Kevin Magill, Stephen Morse, and Paul Russell. As with all of my writing on free will, Robert Kane gave trenchant criticisms and warm encouragement. I also thank two anonymous Oxford University Press readers for incisive commentaries on the submitted draft. I am grateful to all these persons.

I also am happy to thank Diane Harpst and Carrie James for proofreading the manuscript, the Pennsylvania State System Faculty Professional Development Council for funding in the summer of 1994, the editor of *Philosophical Studies* for permission to use parts of my "How to Frame the Free Will Problem" (1994), and the editor of *The Southern Journal of Philosophy* for permission to use parts of my "The Principle of Rational Explanation Defended" (1993). Finally, Cynthia Read and the staff at Oxford University Press were tremendously helpful in bringing this book into existence.

Edinboro, Pennsylvania   R. D.
February 1996

Contents

1 Introduction, 3
   1. Free Will Subjectivism and Metaphilosophy, 3
   2. An Example of the Importance of Metaphilosophy, 8
   3. A Provisional Definition of *Free Choice*, 10
   4. Overview of the Book, 12

I THE FREE WILL PROBLEM AS A PROBLEM
   IN METAPHILOSOPHY

2 Metaphilosophies, 17
   1. What Is Philosophy *For*?, 17
   2. Desires-for-Philosophy and Conceptions of Philosophy, 19
   3. Four Metaphilosophies, 22
   4. The Importance of Having a Metaphilosophy, 32
   5. The Unprovability of Metaphilosophy: Two Reasons, 33
   6. Three Objections to the Relativity of Metaphilosophies, 37
   7. Conclusion, 39

3 Intermediate-Level Philosophical Principles, 40
   1. Five Pairs of Intermediate Principles, 40
   2. The Unprovability of Intermediate-Level Principles, 47
   3. The Interplay of Metaphilosophies, Intermediate Principles,
      and Lower-Level Theories, 49
   4. Why Adopt Philosophy as Continuous with Science?, 53
   5. Conclusion, 55

4 How the Free Will Debate Depends on Metaphilosophy (I), 56
   1. Reasons for Believing in Free Will, 56
   2. The Burden-of-Proof Issue, 60

3. How Far May Philosophers 'Go' to Accommodate
   Free Will?, 62
4. Strawson's Subjectivist Account of Blame, 63
5. The Debate over Dual Rationality, 69

5 How the Free Will Debate Depends on Metaphilosophy (II), 77
   1. The Analogy between the Metaphysics of Ethics and
      the Metaphysics of Free Will, 78
   2. Van Inwagen's Consequence Argument, 82
   3. Frankfurt's Principle of Alternative Possibilities, 86
   4. Is Equal Proof Needed in All Areas of Philosophy?, 90
   5. Standard and Non-Standard Views of Moral Responsibility, 93
   6. Conclusion, 96

II FREE WILL FROM THE PERSPECTIVE OF PHILOSOPHY
   AS CONTINUOUS WITH SCIENCE

6 How to Frame the Free Will Problem, 99
   1. A Radical Approach to Free Will, 100
   2. Four Free Will Theories, 101
   3. Another Theory, 103
   4. Conclusion, 108

7 The Fragmentation of Free Will, 109
   1. The Unity Objection, 110
   2. The Fragmentation-Is-No-Problem Objection, 111
   3. Two Preliminary Reasons to Reject Both Types of
      the Fragmentation-Is-No-Problem Objection, 112
   4. Reasons to Reject the *Bald* Example, 114
   5. Reasons to Reject Cockburn's Move, 119
   6. Mele's Objection, 122
   7. Conclusion, 124

8 *Free Will* Is a Moral Concept, 126
   1. What Does It Mean to Call *Free Choice* a Moral Term?, 127

2. A Preliminary Reason for Thinking That
   Free Choice Is Moral, 128
3. The Open-Question Argument: *Goodness* and *Freeness*, 130
4. The Analogy with Moral Facts: Freeness Facts
   Have No Explanatory Power, 132
5. The Goodness of Ultimacy, 134
6. The Dispute over Magnanimity, 138
7. Conclusion, 142

9 Hume's Principle: The Subjectivity of Moral
   Responsibility and Free Will, 143
   1. Defining the Key Terms, 144
   2. Why Hume's Principle Implies That Ascriptions
      of *Moral Responsibility* Cannot Be True, 147
   3. Why Hume's Principle Implies That *Free Choice*
      Is a Moral Concept, 151
   4. Conclusion, 154

10 Conclusion, 156
   1. Where We Are, 156
   2. Philosophical Consequences, 158
   3. Consequences for Persons, 161

References, 167
Index, 173

METAPHILOSOPHY AND FREE WILL

1

Introduction

1. Free Will Subjectivism and Metaphilosophy

There cannot be any such thing as free will, and there cannot be any such thing as moral responsibility either. Determinism has nothing to do with it, because the difficulty lies solely in the ideas of free will and moral responsibility. Our proclaiming choices to be free and persons to be morally responsible for their choices can be nothing more than our venting of non-truth-valued attitudes, none of which is 'more correct' or 'more rational' than competing attitudes about choices and persons. Nihilism regarding attitudes defeats all theories that hold that *free will* and *moral responsibility* are coherent, objective concepts. This is the view that I believe is true, the view that I argue for in the second part of this book, and argued for in *The Non-Reality of Free Will* (Double, 1991B). I have come to believe, however, that on grounds of logical consistency the subjectivist variety of free will non-realism that I think is true cannot support itself in a decisive way.

No matter how impressive an argument for a free will position may be, that argument can always be stalemated. For this reason, anyone who argues for any position on free will needs to ask why the free will problem remains so completely intractable despite the efforts of many of the ablest thinkers in the history of philosophy. The explanation I provide in the first part of this book undermines the attempt to establish *any* free will theory, including my own subjectivist answer. Hence, I do not purport to show that the theory that I believe *is* true is more worthy of acceptance than all competing theories. If I am right, other theorists cannot show that theirs are best either.

Although I try in part II to support subjectivism the best I can, my most important thesis is that disputes over free will are in principle unsolvable because opposing theorists hold different meta-level views that support their answers to the problem. These include metaphilosophies and intermediate-level philosophical principles. By a *metaphilosophy* I mean a view of what philosophy is, what philosophy can do, and, especially, what philosophy is *for*. As I show in chapter 2, metaphilosophies depend on our desires-for-philosophy, which are various, and none of which is better than the rest. Because we cannot say that any desire-for-philosophy is objectively best, we cannot say that any metaphilosophy is objectively best. Our metaphilosophies give support to and receive support from correlative intermediate-level principles, such as our views about the fact/value distinction or the importance of ontological sparseness in philosophical theory construction. These principles cannot be proved to be more reasonable than their competitors, nor are they plausible or implausible per se; they can be assessed only in terms of their connections to metaphilosophies on the one hand and lower-level philosophical theories on the other.

Certain combinations of metaphilosophical views and supporting intermediate principles make plausible some accounts of free will, and other combinations make plausible opposing accounts. Thus, any argument for or against a specific free will position—such as compatibilism, incompatibilism, or subjectivism—will be persuasive only if we hold an appropriate metaphilosophy and set of intermediate philosophical principles. Because our free will theories depend on these non-objective, psychologically driven views, it turns out that no free will theory can be shown to be more reasonable than its competitors.

If we accept the metaphilosophical views that drive subjectivism, then we believe that there *can be* no single philosophical viewpoint that all rational and impartial persons would have to adopt and from which they would see that one free will theory is more plausible than the rest. Instead of a single 'correct' viewpoint, there would be many, depending on the meta-level positions we adopt; none of these positions could be shown to be objectively best, because their plausibility would depend on subjective facts about us. Thus, no solution to the free will problem could be shown to be correct—not even the one that *is* correct—because the selection of a viewpoint from which to appreciate the strength of a free will theory depends on our non-truth-valued desires.

I draw several conclusions from this. First, we can 'justify' specific free will theories only relative to our metaphilosophies and intermediate principles. Rather than arguing that, for example, compatibilism is most plausible per se, we must say that assuming one combination of metaphilosophy and intermediate principles, compatibilism is most plausible, but that assuming another family of views, compatibilism is not. Second, a good deal of analytical work may be done in order to argue that the package that we prefer coheres more harmoniously than another. Much of the free will literature can be reinterpreted as attempts to show the attractiveness of various packages of metaphilosophy, intermediate principles, and specific theories. Third, because most of us presuppose our metaphilosophical views without explicitly stating them (and assume that our interlocutors share them), we typically are unaware of the role that metaphilosophy plays in supporting our substantive views. Once we recognize this, we may not only better understand the gridlock in the free will debate but also better appreciate the reasoning provided from all sides.

These points may look wildly relativistic or even anti-philosophical. Am I saying that one of the paradigmatic problems of philosophy can be nothing more than rhetoric, an area where theories cannot be assessed rationally? Am I saying that different free will 'language games' are incommensurable and that there is no way of stepping outside our views to assess their plausibility?

I respond in two ways. First, I am not an anti-philosopher in any fashionable 'postmodern' sense. The thesis of this book relies on traditional philosophical themes that are anathema to postmodernists (e.g., the fact/value distinction, the correspondence theory of truth, and the belief that some theories more accurately describe reality than others). I make recommendations for revising a small part of the philosophical enterprise, but I do not reject it. I think that philosophy's traditional metaphysical questions are eminently worthy of our best intellectual efforts.

I view the ontology of value as an important metaphysical issue. With respect to this issue, which I believe is pivotal to both ethics and the free will problem, I am a values subjectivist. I hold that there are no objective evaluational facts lying outside of the cognitions of conscious beings who make the evaluations. I think that the adoption of value subjectivism forces us to naturalize those areas of philosophy that presuppose value realism. A subjectivist view of moral properties leaves normative ethics with no subject matter except social science (psychology, sociology, anthropology, and sociobiology). Analogously, a subjectivism of free will and moral responsibility eclipses the standard free will debate, because there is nothing objective for the disputants to analyze. Free will naturalized, like normative ethics naturalized, becomes a matter of feelings and attitudes—in this case, our feelings about autonomy, dignity, moral responsibility, reactive attitudes, remorse, and related topics.

As a metaphysical realist, I believe that there is a way the world is outside of our cognitions. (We might say with Robert Kane [1993] that the world is the sum of the *many* ways that it is, but this claim also takes the world to be an entity that we cannot influence by our cognitions.) By my lights, distinguishing between the world and our representations of the world is all we need to do in order to be metaphysical realists. The only other alternative—ontologically rather than epistemologically speaking—is idealism, which I take to be implausible, though not refutable. This combination of metaphysical realism applied to the non-moral and subjectivism applied to the moral may be mistaken for a view that is fashionably postmodern, but it is really a species of old-fashioned, dull, unhip naturalism.

Here is my second point. For me, metaphysical realism contains no commitments regarding our knowledge of reality; this view differs from that of some realists (Boyd, 1988, 181) who include within their conception of realism the claim that we possess the methods to obtain knowledge. Thus, the relativism of my view is a relativism that applies to our attempt to *know* the best solution to the free will problem, not to the question of the *existence* of free will, which I reject. Consider an issue where realism obtains if it ever does: the question of whether indeterminism or determinism is the case. According to metaphysical realism, this is a question of how the world is, beyond our power to add or detract. But our *choice* of which factors to weigh in our decision whether to add determinism to our stock of philosophical beliefs is an exercise of practical rather than theoretical reason.

In order to avoid dogmatism, we need to be aware of any factor that might be relevant to our decision, whether epistemic or non-epistemic. The factors we elect to weigh in our decision about whether to accept determinism depend in large part on what we desire to accomplish by our investigation. For instance, we may decide to make our sole aim *fact-tracking* (Robert Nozick's 1981 term) or, as I shall express it, *truth-tracking*. Or we may allow ourselves to be influenced by how beneficial to human well-being we think the two alternative beliefs are. If we think that determinism has morally repugnant consequences, and if we think that moral considerations should play a role in what we let into our belief stockpile, we may decide to pitch our standards for accepting determinism at a higher level than we would if we thought that determinism lacks such consequences or if we did not allow morality such a gatekeeper function. Hence, although the issue of whether determinism obtains is an objective fact immune to the influence of our beliefs about it, our acceptance or rejection of determinism depends on our values. So, our decision concerning a purely factual thesis ultimately depends on our values, which we subjectivists believe are non-truth-tracking attitudinal states.

Here is a slightly different way to express this point. There are two questions, both important, that need to be distinguished: (i) What theory of reality is most likely to be true relative to our epistemic condition, irrespective of any non-epistemic factors we may choose to weigh in arriving at our worldview? (ii) What theory of reality should we hold, all things considered, epistemic and non-epistemic factors taken into account? Even if we think that only question (i) and not question (ii) is worthy of the attention of philosophers, question (ii) will not go away. As practical beings, we need to address it. *If* we decide that philosophers, qua philosophers, do not speak to question (ii), *then* the further question would arise: Should we, as practical agents, accept the verdicts to philosophical problems produced by our best philosophical (i.e., epistemic) efforts? This means that the question of whether we should let epistemic considerations be the sole arbiter of our beliefs about the world is not an epistemic question but a question of value.

The way the world is is the world's business. The theory of the world we adopt is our business. Any exercise of theoretical reason in arriving at beliefs involves an exercise of practical reason, which depends on our values, desires, aspirations, and fears, as well as our beliefs. Thus, our picture of reality is a function of facts and values. Even if we elect to take the purely truth-tracking route, our final picture depends on our decision to do so, which manifests our decision that the truth-tracking method is more valuable than the all-things-considered method. *If* we add the premise of value non-realism, we arrive at belief relativism, which I combine with metaphysical realism: There is a way the world is, but because our strategies for finding out depend on evaluations that are neither true nor false, we can never have a truth-tracking proof that we have got the right answer.

Suppose that the world *is* a certain way irrespective of human cognition—that the world's intrinsic properties are completely independent of our attempt to know what they are like. This supposition of metaphysical realism is consistent with a complete epistemological skepticism that denies that we know anything about the way the world is. For even if the world is a thing in itself, knowable at all or totally unknowable, the world's structure has no way to impose itself on thinkers who hold conflicting beliefs about it and force them into agreement. Conceptual relativists such as Hilary Putnam (1987) and Richard Rorty (1993) note that human beings are always free to adopt incommensurable conceptual schemes. For these thinkers, this establishes that *reality* is relative to our conceptual schemes. Such arguments astound me. These arguments cannot get started if we separate metaphysics and epistemology, and for one who holds the metaphilosophical view I do, it is axiomatic to distinguish between the question of what exists and the question of our knowledge of what exists. These relativist arguments may undermine our claim to know the precise nature of reality, as if we needed argumentation to prove that; but they do not 'relativize' anything beyond our knowledge if we distinguish between metaphysics and epistemology.

Here is my argument regarding metaphilosophies:

1. The philosophical conclusions we reach about the world (as opposed to the way the world is) depend on the practical reasoning by which we decide what to count as evidence for our conclusions.
2. Practical reasoning depends on desires as well as beliefs.
3. Desires cannot *be shown* to be true, nor can they be shown to be better or worse (according to us subjectivists, because desires cannot *be* true or better or worse).
4. Therefore, the philosophical conclusions we reach cannot be shown to be true, nor can they be shown to be better or worse (according to us subjectivists, cannot be true or better or worse).

2. An Example of the Importance of Metaphilosophy

Let me offer an illustration to preview my thesis on the importance of metaphilosophy to our substantive views regarding free will. In some introductory philosophy anthologies, the free will selections are placed in the ethics section, and in others they are placed in the metaphysics or philosophy of mind section. To some extent, this can be explained by imputing to anthologists the belief that the existence of free will is an ontological matter that has moral implications. But the inclusion of free will under each heading also reveals differences in how philosophers understand the free will problem. Some philosophers take free will to be *primarily* a problem of moral philosophy and take the same approach to the free will problem that they do with moral philosophy. On the other side, some philosophers view free will as primarily a question of ontology and apply to it the methodology they think appropriate to questions about what exists.

If all philosophers used the same methodology for questions in all areas of philosophy, it would not matter whether some see free will as a problem in moral philosophy and others see it as a problem in metaphysics. They would approach the problem the same way. But different philosophers approach philosophical problems in vastly different ways. Consider the views that might be taken by someone who sees the free will problem as a question in ethics and someone who sees it as a question in metaphysics. Many moral philosophers think that the proper method for distinguishing between morally just and unjust social arrangements is by using John Rawls's (1971) method of reflective equilibrium, where we test general principles against our specific moral intuitions until we reach a balance, never broaching questions in the metaphysics of ethics. Many of the philosophers who take free will to be an issue in moral philosophy believe that reflective equilibrium is the proper way to figure out what factors enable us to be free and morally responsible, without needing to broach questions in the metaphysics of free will. In each case, the difference between the moral and the immoral and the free and the unfree is assumed, and the only question asked is how to tell which is which. (See Fischer, 1994, 151, for a candid application of reflective equilibrium to the free will problem.)

Contrast this to an approach that sees free will as a metaphysical problem. One (but only one) way to approach metaphysics is by a methodology of extreme ontological frugality that treats every candidate for admission into our ontology as needing ontological (not moral, not aesthetic, not practical) justification. Such an approach, which I apply in part II of this book, takes the foundational questions very seriously: How can there *be* free will? Where *is* the property that makes choices free? *How* could moral responsibility exist in a naturalistic cosmos? We are likely to use vastly different principles for evaluating arguments in the free will discussion, depending on which of these two perspectives we adopt.

3. A Provisional Definition of *Free Choice*

I want to emphasize what my subjectivist non-realism does not deny. By *free will* I do not include political freedoms such as those protected by the Bill of Rights in the U.S. Constitution (e.g., freedoms of speech, religion, press, and assembly), which can be stipulatively defined and clearly instanced. Nor am I concerned with the kinds of freedom that compatibilists decisively have shown that we can have, provided we are able to act as we choose (Hobbes) or choose as we reflectively think we ought (Frankfurt, 1971). I *am* concerned with the freedom of choice that is supposed to be necessary if persons are to deserve praise and blame for their actions, to be morally responsible agents, and to warrant the whole range of reactive attitudes (P. Strawson, 1962) such as resentment, indignation, and gratitude that mark our commonsense way of viewing other persons *as persons*. Free will also is supposed to underwrite a type of dignity and autonomy that could not be enjoyed by beings who lack free will. This morally laden type of freedom is what incompatibilists believe cannot exist if determinism is true and compatibilists must show can exist even if all choices are determined if they are to answer the incompatibilists' worries about determinism. I am a subjectivist about *this* kind of free will.

Although I argue in part II that *free will* has no objective reference, we still need a working definition of the concept. Unsurprisingly, there is no standard definition of the term even for provisional use. A familiar definition defines *free choices* to be uncaused libertarian choices of the sort that incompatibilists believe we need in order to be morally responsible for our behavior. Despite the advantage of precedent (van Inwagen, 1983; Honderich, 1988 and 1993), this approach faces decisive objections. First, this approach encourages the confusion that the incompatibilist view of free will can be made true by stipulation. Second, although all libertarian accounts of free choice posit an uncaused element at some time before the choice, there is no consensus on when it occurs. Some theorists locate the uncaused event in the occurrence of the psychological states that precede the choice (Dennett, 1984), others locate it at the moment of choice alone (van Inwagen, 1983; Clarke, 1993), and others locate it at both places (Kane, 1985). Other libertarians believe that free choices may be determined in their immediate histories so long as they can be traced back to a *prior* uncaused choice (Kane, 1996). So even if we wanted to create a bias against compatibilism by defining *free choice* in terms of a specific libertarian account, that definition would count against other libertarians as well as the compatibilists.

I define *free choice* in a placeholder fashion that is neutral between competing theories of what a free choice is. I see this as analogous to functionalist definitions of mental terms that leave open the question of whether mental states are physical or nonphysical. Let us define *free choices* as *choices that, unless some excusing condition obtains, are sufficient to qualify their agents as morally responsible for the actions those choices (immediately) produce and as warranting reactive attitudes.* This definition is neutral between competing theories of what free will is. It shows the connection between moral issues and free will that I believe is the point behind worrying about free will in the first place. By doing so, it highlights the internal tension in the concept of *free choice*— a tension that will eventually enable us to dispute the concept's claim to denote anything outside of the subjective predilections of users of the term.

Not all philosophers are convinced that free will, perhaps even varieties of it that interest philosophers, has much to do with moral responsibility. Thinkers such as Bruce Waller (1990 and in correspondence) and Kevin Magill (forthcoming) note that there are valuable types of freedom that are not morally laden. Moreover, much of the subjectivist argument of part II assumes that we pin down free will by its connection to moral responsibility. So it seems that this premise needs defense generally and, in particular, because my subjectivist reasoning depends on it.

As one might suspect, I have a metaphilosophical response. Although we may elect to care about anything we like under the rubric of free will, perhaps the majority of philosophers who have written about free will have believed that justifying moral responsibility (including the expression of reactive attitudes, blame, and punishment) is 'the prize' that constitutes the point of caring about free will. This certainly is my view. Using notions I develop in chapter 2, if we approach the free will problem from the metaphilosophical perspective of Praxis (supporting human well-being), Underpinning Commonsense Beliefs, or Worldview Construction, then we care about free will primarily due to our interest in whether moral responsibility can be supported. If this is what brings us to the free will problem, then even if we can explicate senses of freedom that are not inseparably connected to moral responsibility, we still will want to ask the further question of whether moral responsibility can exist.

In *Freedom without Responsibility*, for instance, Waller gives two independent arguments: one to show that freedom is compatible with naturalism and another to show that moral responsibility is not compatible with naturalism. Waller cares very much about moral responsibility; he hopes to exorcise it. But if we care about the possibility of moral responsibility anyway, then we do Waller no injustice by following tradition and drawing an explicit connection between free will and moral responsibility. This approach makes free will vulnerable to arguments against the possibility of moral responsibility but does not damage Waller's view—there still will be those other varieties of freedom that Waller cares about that are not put at risk. *If* we think that moral responsibility is the prize, then it does not matter whether we define free will in terms of it or not. We will have to get around to moral responsibility eventually.

On the other hand, one can approach the free will problem *without* caring about moral responsibility. If we hold certain metaphilosophical views, we may feel no need to connect free will with responsibility. Philosophers who want philosophy to underpin science may be uninterested in moral topics but may care about freedom as a theoretical construct in psychology—for example, as something that persons with high perceived control manifest more frequently than do persons with low perceived control (E. Skinner, 1995). Philosophers who see philosophy at its best as a stimulating literary genre (Philosophy as Conversation) may find moral responsibility a boring and outmoded theologically inspired form of conversation. One theme of this book is that according to the metaphilosophy I endorse, we cannot legislate what motivations philosophers 'should' bring to philosophical problems. Another theme is that the substantive conclusions on free will we reach (such as my subjectivism) will be relative to those unlegislatable motivations.

4. Overview of the Book

Part I develops the connection between metaphilosophy and free will. In chapter 2 I elaborate four metaphilosophies that drive different answers to questions in the free will problem. I also argue that no metaphilosophy can be proven to be better than its competitors. In chapter 3, I provide five pairs of intermediate-level philosophical principles that are particularly relevant to our thinking about free will. These also are not provable. In chapters 4 and 5 I provide ten applications from recent free will debates that demonstrate metaphilosophical differences that make the free will problem unsolvable.

Part II applies the metaphilosophy I call *Philosophy as Continuous with Science* to the free will problem. In chapter 6 I describe how the free will problem looks to an advocate of that metaphilosophy. Chapter 7 argues that relative to that metaphilosophy, free choice of the sort that is supposed to justify moral responsibility 'fragments' into varieties of free will, none of which has a strong claim to exist. Chapter 8 shows that free will is a moral concept, which defeats its claim to denote according to the value subjectivism that is implicit in Philosophy as Continuous with Science. Chapter 9 argues that if we accept the Humean principle of the non-derivability of moral statements from non-moral ones, we will be able to prove both moral subjectivism and free will subjectivism. Chapter 10 considers where we are left if we accept the arguments of this book.

In recent years several philosophers have noted that the free will problem involves attitudes. Peter Strawson (1962), Peter Unger (1984), Thomas Nagel (1986), and Ted Honderich (1988; 1993) see the problem as one of perplexity over which attitudes we should adopt toward persons if we believe that all choices are determined. Relative to *my* meta-level views, I do not believe that these brilliant thinkers have taken their awareness of the attitudinal nature of the free will problem to its best conclusion.

I can make no clear sense of talk about appropriate and inappropriate attitudes. This distinguishes my view from all the others: I think that talk about free will in the moral-responsibility-justifying sense defined above is so much verbiage, a kind of A. J. Ayer–like booing and hurrahing. Because I deny that free will makes objective sense, my subjectivist non-realism is quite different from that of non-realists who use other grounds to deny that free will can exist. For instance, hard determinists argue that free will does not exist, but they use an objective incompatibilistic premise to do so. Galen Strawson (1986; 1994) denies that there can be free will because we cannot perform the logically impossible task of self-creation. I deny that free will makes even this much sense.

For readers of *The Non-Reality of Free Will*, I should say how this book differs from my previous book. The earlier book was concerned solely with providing a negative answer to the question of whether free will and moral responsibility can exist. I remain concerned with this question and try to give better arguments than I used in that book. The difference is that when I wrote the first book I did not understand the extent to which the plausibility of philosophical theories depends on metaphilosophical factors, nor that on my own subjectivist principles, this makes argumentation about free will wildly relativistic. I find this a sobering, but, given my fondness for sobering facts, gratifying discovery.

I

THE FREE WILL PROBLEM AS
A PROBLEM IN METAPHILOSOPHY

2
Metaphilosophies

In this chapter, I explicate my notion of a metaphilosophy and illustrate the differences in metaphilosophies that I claim make the free will problem unsolvable. In section 1, I place the question of metaphilosophy within the broader context of asking for the purposes of human activities in general. In section 2, I show that our view of philosophy influences, but does not determine, our metaphilosophy. Section 3 elaborates four metaphilosophies that I call *Philosophy as Conversation, Philosophy as Praxis, Philosophy as Underpinnings,* and *Philosophy as Worldview Construction.* Section 4 shows how having a metaphilosophy can be helpful in philosophical debate. Section 5 shows why metaphilosophies cannot be proven. Section 6 anticipates three objections to the thesis of the previous section.

1. What Is Philosophy *For*?

A human activity is *for* whatever we want it to be for. This reflects not only the truism that practical reason depends on our desires as well as our beliefs but also the Sartrean fact that we give ourselves our own purposes. Given the number of desires we have, we perform activities for indefinitely many goals. Even a rarified intellectual activity such as science, art, or philosophy can be done for many goals: pleasure, the exercise of creativity, spiritual consolation, intellectual stimulation, the pursuit of truth, artistic expression, the attempt to gain insight into human nature, venting one's spleen, or galvanizing others to moral action, as well as the more mundane aims, such as gaining money or fame. Finding out what an artificer intends an artifact to be for is easy in principle, but determining 'the' unique goal of a complex human activity pursued by many persons is impossible because of the number of goals we value. Establishing 'the correct' goal of such an activity involves a second sort of impossibility beyond that created by the multiplicity of goals, because of the evaluative character of *correct*.

In my department there is a perennial debate. In our ethics classes shall we teach moral theory or contemporary moral issues? Should we demand a lot of homework from our majors, or should we demand less so they can work long hours for the Young Socialists club? How many logic vs. cultural pluralism courses should there be in the university's general education requirements? These are difficult questions because they are particularized versions of this more fundamental question: What do we want to contribute to our students' educations? And this question leads to a still more basic question: What is education *for*? Given that this is an imperfect world, where we labor under limitations of time, energy, and intellectual resources, the question can be framed this way: Should we be more interested in making our students *smart* or *good*? This is a paradigmatic value judgment.

The question of what philosophy is for has parallels in art and science. In *The Republic*, Plato argued that art is for making us morally better persons, that is, art ought to provide lessons in morality. Many Renaissance artists believed that the purpose of art is the glorification of God. Other artists thought that art's purpose is to enable us to glimpse truths that are not discernible in other ways: "Truth is beauty and beauty, truth." A more popular view takes the point of art to lie not in revealing truths but in providing new ways of looking at things and in expressing and evoking feelings. Here we have four different proposals. Art is for promulgating morality, for glorifying God, for ascertaining truths not otherwise determinable, and for enriching our lives irrespective of morality, God, and truth.

Even among scientists, among whom we would expect greater consensus, there are important disputes over what science is for. Science can be viewed as a theoretical attempt to discover the hidden causes of all phenomena, as the effort to unravel the deep mysteries of the cosmos. This view of science, in the hands of the optimist, gives us scientific realism (Galileo), and in the hands of the pessimist it gives us skepticism and even despair (Einstein). Science also can be viewed as a practical aid to technology, by showing us how to predict the course of our sense experience without assuming that its theories are accurate to a deep and hidden microstructure of pure being. This view of science leads to scientific instrumentalism (Mach).

Our decision as to what philosophy is for depends both on what we believe philosophy can accomplish and on what we desire to accomplish by philosophizing. As with practical reason, beliefs and desires are crucial. Just as we do not decide to do actions that we do not believe we can perform, ordinarily we do not decide that philosophy is for an end that we do not believe it can accomplish. So, some philosophers want philosophy to do different things than other philosophers do because they have different beliefs about what philosophy *can* achieve. In particular, some philosophers assign philosophy less ambitious roles than others do simply because the former think philosophy cannot accomplish as much as the latter do.

Different beliefs about what philosophy can do, however, are only part of the story. In philosophy, as in art and science, incompatible answers to the "what is it for" question are driven not only by our different beliefs about what can be accomplished but also by our differing interests, temperaments, values, and desires. Just as our beliefs do not fix our desires generally, our beliefs about what philosophy can accomplish do not fix our desires for what we want philosophy to accomplish. For any complex human activity, what we think it is for depends on what we want to get out of it, and this presupposes a value judgment, as instanced in my department's debate over the goal of education. Just as there are many possible purposes of art and science that are driven by our non-doxastic states, there are many answers to the question of what philosophy's purpose is. Various philosophers want philosophy to serve different purposes simply because philosophers have different values. The metaphilosophy we endorse depends not only on our beliefs but also on our desires-for-philosophy, which depend on non-doxastic states. As Bertrand Russell (1966, 112) quotes William James, "The history of philosophy is to a great extent that of a certain clash of human temperaments."

2. Desires-for-Philosophy and Conceptions of Philosophy

Not only are our desires-for-philosophy underdetermined by our beliefs about what philosophy can do, they are underdetermined by our beliefs about what philosophy *is*. We can agree what little league baseball is but differ about what little league baseball is for. (For having fun, for developing athletic skills, for teaching children how to interact with other children, for developing moral virtues, for pursuing a type of human excellence, and so on.) Likewise, we can agree to a large extent on what philosophy *is*, while disputing what philosophy is *for*. Philosophers who agree that Kant, Plato, and Hume are philosophers and that the existence of minds, God, and universals are philosophical problems can nonetheless disagree over what philosophy is for.

Although our conception of philosophy does not fix our metaphilosophy, in giving a metaphilosophy we presuppose a vision of philosophy. We cannot decide what anything is for without having an idea of what it is like. The question of what philosophy is provides a needed starting point for our inquiry into what philosophy is for, even if it will not give us the endpoint. Interestingly, our decision as to what philosophy is for indirectly affects our decision of what philosophy is.

So far I have claimed that: (i) Our metaphilosophy depends on what we believe philosophy can accomplish. (ii) Our metaphilosophy depends on what we desire that philosophy accomplish, which is influenced by that belief but is not determined by it. (iii) Our metaphilosophy presupposes a vision of what philosophy is and is influenced by it but is not fixed by it. I support these three claims by presenting my view of philosophy and demonstrating the connection between that vision and the metaphilosophy I endorse.

I characterize philosophy for my introductory students by providing an equation. Philosophy, I say, equals a certain subject matter that is addressed with a certain methodology. I portray the subject matter of philosophy as questions that *have* answers (but have not been answered); that *cannot* be answered by science, faith, or common sense; and are of perennial intellectual interest to humans. I represent the methodology as critical thinking, which includes both intellectual and temperamental traits. Primary among the intellectual traits of the critical thinker is careful attention to meaning, especially to understanding what the questions and their answers mean, mapping all possible alternative answers to the questions, and canvassing all the considerations one can imagine that might lend support to one view over another. Among temperamental traits are the desire to see things clearly, the willingness to follow lines of reasoning that may be contrary to one's own beliefs, the desire to evaluate fairly all competing views, and a readiness to suspend judgment, even on our longtime views, when we cannot provide reasons that support one position over another.

This characterization of philosophy generates understandable puzzlement. If philosophy really attempts to answer questions that go beyond science, common sense, and religious faith, how could it possibly succeed? Surely, my students think, these three exhaust our ways of knowing anything. There simply is no *room* for a special fourth kind of knowledge, unless philosophy is truly mystical. But how can philosophy be mystical and still claim to use the methodology of critical thinking?

I do my best to assuage this worry by comparing philosophical theory construction to theory construction designed to answer very difficult, unsettled questions in physical and social science (e.g., whether the known universe will continue to expand indefinitely or contract on itself, and what caused the American Civil War). In doing so I give a sketch of inference to the best explanation, calling it the common denominator of science, philosophy, and the best of commonsense reasoning. I concede that because of the abstract nature of philosophical questions, and because conflicting theories have received brilliant defenses from first-rate philosophers, *philosophical knowledge* is largely a misnomer. Philosophy, I say, is a fallibilistic enterprise that does not purport to arrive at knowledge but hopes to approximate a true picture of the way the world is, making no pretense of being able to *prove* that the world is that way. Plausible belief, not knowledge, is the most that philosophy can hope to obtain. In this sense philosophy demonstrates the inadequacies not only of science, faith, and common sense but also of itself.

I confess that when I present this characterization of philosophy to my students I am tempted to suppose that it is uncontroversial at least for Western analytic philosophy. If we look only for confirming instances, one of those congenital cognitive flaws of the human race (Johnson-Laird and Wason, 1977), it is easy to see the great historical figures as providing inductive support for this account. Unhappily, if we try to disconfirm the characterization, we find that it seems to rule out many acknowledged philosophers and branches of philosophy: the Milesians (wrong subject matter), St. Augustine and most of the medievals (wrong temperament), Descartes (wrong temperament), Kant (wrong temperament), Marx (wrong subject matter and wrong temperament), Nietzsche (wrong subject matter and wrong methodology), phenomenology (wrong subject matter and wrong methodology), ordinary language philosophy (wrong subject matter), Richard Rorty and the postmodernists (wrong subject matter and wrong methodology), and all the "philosophy of . . ." areas of contemporary analytic philosophy (wrong subject matter). As innocuous as my account is by my lights, it is unacceptable to those who do not share those lights.

The reason my characterization of philosophy seems both uncontroversial and contentious is that it contains metaphilosophical presuppositions that I can recognize but that I often overlook. First, I claim that philosophy's subject matter is proposing answers to difficult theoretical questions. But this presumes that realistic truth exists and is worthy of our attempts to obtain it, however tenuous our grasp may be. Someone who thinks that realistic truth makes no sense or that even if it makes sense it is not worth seeking cannot accept my claim. Second, my view of philosophy contains no mention of the human condition, let alone any attempt to improve it. This applies both to morality and to our attempt to deal with the non-moral problems of human life, death, and meaning. Third, on my view, philosophy's methodology gives no priority to the preexisting beliefs of common sense, religion, or morality, instead treating all beliefs as equally subject to skeptical scrutiny. Philosophy is cast as an imperious inquisitor of all areas of intellectual life, rather than as a helpful contributor. Fourth, nothing is said about philosophy being aesthetically satisfying, emotionally valuable, or even *interesting*.

All of these points contest either my presuppositions about what philosophy can do or my evaluations about what goals philosophy should pursue. Someone with different beliefs about philosophy or different desires-for-philosophy will end up with a different characterization of philosophy and a different metaphilosophy, even if that person and I would largely agree in our list of the twenty greatest philosophers.

3. Four Metaphilosophies

Metaphilosophies are idealized, abstract characterizations of what philosophy is for. The most important factor behind what philosophers think philosophy is for is their desires-for-philosophy. Because real philosophers have several desires for philosophy, they will seldom fall under just one metaphilosophical category. In addition, what philosophers want from philosophy changes in intensity over time and from problem to problem. Although I quote famous philosophers in this chapter, my purpose is to use their words as *examples* of my taxonomy of metaphilosophical views rather than to claim that those philosophers adhere to those positions in their overall views. I use historical and contemporary philosophers to illustrate my notions of metaphilosophies and leave the interpretations of these philosophers to historians of philosophy, who are better able to perform the task.

Although I see my metaphilosophies as a taxonomy of *possible* motivations, I hope that these four views cover most motivations philosophers *do* bring to the free will problem. They do not purport to cover every possible motivation one could bring to philosophy, such as Philosophy as Flaunting Common Sense or Philosophy as Stirring Controversy. (I owe these examples to an anonymous reader.) One could arrive at different metaphilosophies than just these four. I select the metaphilosophies I do because of my interest in the free will problem; if I were considering a different problem, I might provide a different taxonomy of metaphilosophies.

We can ask a few questions that help subdivide the metaphilosophical terrain. The first concerns whether we see philosophy's value as intrinsic to the activity of philosophizing or depending at least in part on its contribution to an extrinsic goal beyond philosophy. If we answer that philosophy's value is intrinsic, then we need to state what that intrinsic value is. Two answers have been historically most significant: (a) Philosophy's purpose is to seek truth irrespective of any other benefit that might result from the pursuit of truth. (b) Philosophy's aim is to produce interesting modes of intellectual insight without claiming to present truth.

If we claim that philosophy's aim is extrinsic to the activity itself, we will need to specify that aim. Here again two main candidates stand out: (c) Philosophy's purpose is to help make life better, whether by contributing to us as moral beings or by enhancing our ability to cope with nihilism, death, and questions about the meaning of our lives. (d) Philosophy's purpose is to help shore up some other area of our intellectual lives, such as science, religion, or common sense.

I have idealized these four aims. Some advocates of views (c) and (d) will say that they care about truth, and some philosophers will say that they care about both the intrinsic aims of truth-seeking and producing interesting non-truth-seeking literature. This is what we should expect, given the promiscuity of desire. Here are the four metaphilosophies.

Philosophy as Conversation

A first view, which I call Philosophy as Conversation after Richard Rorty (1979; 1989), corresponds to the view of art as non-truth-tracking enrichment, that is, as an activity that contributes to our intellectual lives without pronouncing on the character of ultimate reality. Because a metaphilosophy is fixed by beliefs about philosophy and desires-for-philosophy, we could reach the Conversation position in two ways. We might deny that philosophy can discover realistic truth by providing skeptical arguments or by dismissing the very attempt to find truth. Or we might claim that even if philosophy can discover truth, this goal is not sufficiently valuable relative to the other aims that philosophy might pursue. A Conversation view of philosophy can be reached through a mixture of these routes.

On the Conversation view, philosophy at its best can be intellectually stimulating, but it cannot arrive at any 'deeper' truths about knowledge, existence, and value than can any other literary form. Philosophical work is to be evaluated on the Kierkegaard-like scale of the interesting/boring, rather than the true/false. (I owe this way of putting it to Robert Kane.) Rorty's anti-philosophers, the ironists, "take the writings of all people with poetic gifts, all the original minds who had a talent for redescription—Pythagoras, Plato, Milton, Newton, Goethe, Kant, Kierkegaard, Baudelaire, Darwin, Freud—as grist to be put through the same dialectical mill" (1989, 76). Dissuaded from its past delusions of grandeur, philosophy on this view sees itself simply as what intellectuals do when they engage in discussions about topics that traditionally have been called *philosophical*.

According to this metaphilosophy, all of the following count as philosophical literature: the history of philosophy and the history of ideas; broadly theoretical analyses of society, politics, and culture; aesthetic criticism; philosophical anthropology (i.e., speculative social science, as in Freud, Marx, Comte, and Nietzsche). Other components include: the view that philosophy is a form of literature that portrays the human condition, as in Sartre and Camus, and the view that philosophy is a form of all-purpose critique of society. John Dewey, who also exemplifies my category of Philosophy as Praxis, expresses the idea of philosophy as social critique this way: "[Philosophy's] business is to accept and to utilize for a purpose the best available knowledge of its own time and place. And this purpose is criticism of beliefs, institutions, customs, policies with respect to their bearing upon good" (1926, 407–8).

Dewey also forecasts this role for philosophy: "[T]he task of future philosophy is to clarify men's ideas as to the social and moral strife of their own day" (1948, 26).

Philosophy as Praxis

A second view, Philosophy as Praxis, corresponds to the view of art as contributing to morality by claiming that philosophy should be instrumental in making us better persons. *Better* can be understood as *morally better*, in which case philosophy has a moral function to serve by giving intellectual support to ideological goals or by supporting morality generally. The enhancement of morality is the most important theme behind Praxis. *Better* also can be understood to mean *happier* or *more able to cope with life*, in which case philosophy contributes to our non-moral good—for example, by enabling us to deal with the frustration and despair that can be brought about by science or philosophy. Praxis thinkers may disagree over whether philosophy is capable of finding realistic truths, but the idealized Praxis thinker places philosophy's contribution to human well-being above its aim of truth-seeking. Camus, who exemplifies Philosophy as Conversation as well as Praxis, claims in the first sentence of *The Myth of Sisyphus* that establishing a meaning for human existence is philosophy's greatest task: "There is but one truly serious philosophical problem, and that is suicide" (1955, 1). Philosophers such as Plato and Kant who try to construct metaphysical pictures that make a place for morality exemplify a Praxis motivation.

A classic expression of Praxis is Marx's claim in his eleventh thesis against Feuerbach that *the point* of philosophy is not to *interpret* the world but to *change* it (Feuer, 1959, 245). The idea that philosophy should support sociopolitical movements has been more influential among Continental thinkers than among academic philosophers in English-speaking countries. But there are many examples among the latter that represent the view that philosophy has a moral mission. One is the importance that American pragmatists such as Dewey and James assign to the goal of contributing to human well-being beyond simply constructing pictures of reality. Another is the attempt to underpin liberal democracy, as in John Rawls's *Theory of Justice*. According to Hilary Putnam, Wittgenstein's view of philosophy as 'therapy' also has a moral motivation: "If Wittgenstein wants to make a bonfire of our philosophical vanities, this is not a matter of intellectual sadism; . . . those vanities, in his view, are what keep us from trust and, perhaps even more important, keep us from compassion" (1992, 178–79).

Another example of Praxis motivation comes from philosophers who see an urgency in finding "the place of reason in ethics" in meta-ethics. The moral realist David Brink argues:

> If . . . rejection of moral realism would undermine the nature of existing practices and beliefs, then the metaphysical queerness of moral realism may seem a small price to pay to preserve these practices and beliefs. I am not claiming that the presumption in favor of moral realism could not be over-turned on a posteriori metaphysical grounds. I am claiming only that we could not determine the appropriate reaction to the success of this [Mackie's anti-realism] metaphysical argument until we determined, among other things, the strength of the presumption in favor of moral realism. (1989, 173–74)

In normative ethics, some writers are motivated not simply to describe a theoretically adequate moral theory but to make readers more moral persons. In the free will problem, some thinkers are motivated to 'construct' workable concepts of freedom and moral responsibility from our confused ideas about them in order to make the intellectual world safe for responsibility (Dennett, 1984, chapter 7). In epistemology, Praxis thinkers try to answer skepticism not simply because skepticism is an intellectual riddle but because it is a threat to our moral and spiritual well-being. Thinkers influenced by Praxis motivation sometimes see the claim that philosophy has a distinctive subject matter and methodology as a reactionary maneuver designed to keep philosophers from addressing morally important questions.

Philosophy as Providing Underpinnings: For Common Sense, Religion, the Law, Natural Science, or Special Sciences

A third view, Philosophy as Underpinnings, sees philosophy's proper role as supporting some other area or areas of intellectual interest. One way to arrive at an Underpinnings view is to believe that philosophy has no special truth-determining qualifications that the underpinned area lacks. Another route is to judge that regardless of philosophy's qualifications, the best goal for philosophy is to support that other area. In principle, philosophy can be used to underpin any other area of thought, but historically the major areas have been religion, science, and common sense. During medieval times, a great motivation for doing philosophy was to underpin religion. Since the rise of modern science, most who adopt the Underpinnings metaphilosophy have opted to underpin science or common sense.

The key behind this metaphilosophy is its view that what is being underpinned, although subject to criticism at its borders, is not open to wholesale criticism by philosophy. Thus, philosophy is assigned a subordinate role to the underpinned area. This turns any pure version of Underpinnings unmixed with other metaphilosophies into an extremely unambitious view of philosophy. This diminution of the scope of philosophy is also noticeable when philosophy is used to give support to even narrower areas, such as a special science, aesthetic criticism, law, or political authority.

Although entire books cannot be subsumed entirely under any one metaphilosophy, A. J. Ayer's *Language, Truth, and Logic* largely reflects the view that philosophy has no distinctive subject matter of its own and should serve science by contributing to its conceptual underpinnings. This view was fairly characteristic of the logical positivists generally and probably influences any philosopher who thinks that the philosophy of science, logic, and decision theory are the most important areas of philosophy. These views are characteristic of Philosophy as Underpinning Science.

Philosophy as Underpinning Common Sense sees philosophy's role as protecting common sense *from* radical philosophy and radical science. This is exemplified by defenders of common sense such as Thomas Reid, G. E. Moore, and J. L. Austin. David Lewis, though prepared to depart from commonsensical views in his own metaphysics, nicely characterizes the role of philosophy as systematizing our beliefs: "One comes to philosophy already endowed with a stock of existing opinions. It is not the business of philosophy either to undermine or to justify these preexisting opinions, to any great extent, but only to try to discover ways of expanding them into an orderly system" (1973, 88).

There is a connection between the metaphilosophy of Philosophy as Underpinning Common Sense and the belief that careful linguistic analysis is the best philosophical method. (In the free will discussion, the Underpinnings metaphilosophy holds that our linguistic intuitions about whether persons are free in various thought experiments are decisive trump.) The metaphilosophy describes the *goal* we wish to attain, while the belief endorses a *method* for attaining that goal. In principle the two can part company. We can chart a circuitous path through uncommonsensical metaphysics in order to underpin commonsense beliefs, and using our ordinary language methodology we can 'follow the argument' to uncommonsensical conclusions. But generally the goal of underpinning common sense and the tactic of relying on our linguistic intuitions to solve philosophical problems go together. To connect the two, we need only the premise that ordinary language, by and large, accurately reflects non-linguistic reality. J. L. Austin suggests this in "A Plea for Excuses" by advocating *linguistic phenomenology*:

> [O]ur common stock of words embodies all the distinctions men have found worth drawing, and all the connexions they have found worth making, in the lifetimes of many generations: these surely are likely to be more numerous, more sound, since they have stood up to the long test of the survival of the fittest, and more subtle, at least in all ordinary and reasonably practical matters, than any that you or I are likely to think up in our armchairs of an afternoon. (1970, 182)

Ted Honderich claims that incompatibilists and compatibilists typically think that the free will problem can be settled linguistically:

> Both sides agree that . . . what we have to do is just to see clearly, not get confused, get a good definition of the idea we all share, not get led astray by other philosophers with a doctrinal ax to grind. . . . The question is importantly a linguistic one. What we have to do is analyze 'free' in ordinary English and similar words in other ordinary languages. (1993, 101)

Finally, when legal theorists address philosophical topics in the attempt to rationalize legal decision-making, we can subsume their motivations under both Praxis and Underpinnings. In "Culpability and Control," the legal philosopher Stephen Morse (1994) tries to make explicit and justify the criteria by which jurists ought to accept diminished-capacity excuses, such as those based on threats, addiction, irrationality, and various types of psychological disorders. Morse's enterprise reveals a Praxis motivation on the premise that a rational legal system is a moral good for a society. It reveals an Underpinnings motivation because it accepts the body of historical legal decisions, while trying to support and fine-tune the theory behind the process.

Morse dismisses global philosophical arguments that no one is free because such a conclusion is of no practical use to jurists, who are not interested in placing in doubt the fundamental assumptions of the criminal justice system: "[A]cceptance of the more general argument would require a complete restructuring of our sense of ourselves as responsible agents, our moral practices more generally, and, not least, our system of criminal justice" (1994, 1594).

According to Morse, legal thinkers need specific theories about the kinds of excuses that we should acknowledge. These should provide relevant distinctions, not overall claims that exonerate everyone:

> In sum, trying to underpin control excuses in terms of will or volitional problems or lack of free will is likely to be inaccurate, confusing, rhetorical, or in its best incarnation, a placeholder for a fuller, more adequate theory of excusing conditions. The will and free will are not legal criteria, and agents in the criminal justice system would do well to dispense with employing them in responsibility analysis and attribution. (1994, 1599)

For Morse, the problems raised by the hard determinists and subjectivists are philosophers' problems for which legal thinkers cannot await philosophical resolution. Nor can legal thinkers derive insight from philosophers' global theories and parlay it into the real distinctions that we need to draw once we assume that most of us are responsible most of the time for our behavior. The law has to assume what philosophers place in doubt—that we can act otherwise than we do and that the concepts of *rationality* applied to actions and *fairness* in the demands we place on each other make good sense—all in absence of proof that these assumptions are metaphysically warranted.

Philosophy as Worldview Construction

A final metaphilosophy takes the goal of philosophy to be similar to the scientific realist's view of the aim of science: an attempt to characterize reality as accurately as we can. In this view of philosophy we try to provide, in Thomas Nagel's (1986) expression, "a view from nowhere." This goal can be characterized in terms of *fact-tracking* (Nozick, 1981), *truth-tropic* (Lipton, 1991), or, as in this work, simply *truth-tracking*. Philosophy as Worldview Construction corresponds to the definition of *philosophy* I offered in the previous section. This view presupposes that philosophy can make better or worse approximations to realistic truth and that doing so is its best goal.

Philosophy as Worldview Construction is the most ambitious view of philosophy, where philosophers take themselves to be providing the most-likely-to-be-true answers to philosophical problems by addressing the hard questions that are either begged or ignored by all other areas of human thought. Practitioners of this view sometimes recommend sweeping and unusual proposals such as solipsism, Platonism, skepticism, idealism, theodicy, the coherence theory of truth, eliminative materialism, and agent causation.

I draw an important distinction between two types of Philosophy as Worldview Construction. If we think that the way to construct the most-likely-to-be-true picture of the world is to emulate a parsimonious scientific view of theory construction, then we exemplify a view I call Philosophy as Continuous with Science. This metaphilosophy correlates with several intermediate philosophical principles I discuss in the next chapter: demanding epistemological scruples, a realist interpretation of theories, a stingy ontology based on inference to the best explanation, and the fact-value distinction. One hero for someone who likes Philosophy as Continuous with Science is Wilfrid Sellars, who claimed that science is the measure of all things and that philosophy needs to try to legitimate the Manifest Image of Man in terms of the Scientific Image of Man. Another is W. V. O. Quine, who argues that everything we admit to our worldview beyond our sensory impressions is a *posit* to be justified only on the grounds of explanatory necessity. Philosophy as Continuous with Science has been derisively labeled *Scientism* (Rorty, 1989; Putnam, 1992; Sorell, 1994).

Philosophy as Continuous with Science is different from Philosophy as Underpinning Science because they have different views of philosophy's scope. Advocates of the former believe that philosophy is for addressing the big questions that go beyond science, common sense, and religion, inasmuch as that metaphilosophy is a species of Philosophy as Worldview Construction. Such thinkers believe that it is a matter of contingent fact that a certain parsimonious view of science—admittedly not shared by all philosophers of science—is the best model for philosophers to use in addressing those questions. In contrast, the idealized advocate of Philosophy as Underpinning Science assigns philosophy a subordinate role and looks askance at such grandiose aims.

Suppose a team of Underpinning Science philosophers and a team of Philosophy as Continuous with Science philosophers went on a field trip to a planet with bizarre, perhaps-sentient creatures who revealed no trace of science or technology. *Relative to that planet*, the former could not ply their trade, there being no science to underpin. *Relative to that planet*, the latter could ply their trade by applying to the scienceless creatures on that planet their conception of good philosophical method extrapolated from the elements of Earthling science they admire. The Philosophy as Continuous with Science team could deal with the mind-body problem, personal identity, and free will problems as they apply to those strange beings.

Not all advocates of Philosophy as Worldvew Construction, however, adopt Philosophy as Continuous with Science. To emphasize the contrast with the former, I call this subset of Philosophy as Worldvew Construction Philosophy as Non-Continuous with Science. Thinkers who adopt this view may have different ideas about science, or, more importantly, may believe that science on any interpretation is not the best model for philosophical theory construction. In addition, Philosophy as Non-Continuous with Science thinkers may assign weight to various non-truth-tracking considerations that are important to the other metaphilosophies. For someone who is pulled by Praxis concerns, this may take the form of giving extra weight to parts of the worldview that appear conducive to moral desiderata. Kant called such considerations *aspirations* (1965, The Canon of Pure Reason, *The Critique of Pure Reason*, A805–B833). For those who feel that the beauty of a philosophical theory or its contribution to underpinning some other area has a role to play in qualifying it for our picture of reality, Conversation or Underpinnings metaphilosophies may influence Worldview Construction.

J. R. Lucas suggests that if we accept a realistic theory of truth, we can no longer select free will theories according to their pragmatic value. Expressed in my terms, this means that accepting realistic truth prevents us (psychologically or morally) from adopting Philosophy as Praxis or Philosophy as Non-Continuous with Science with a Praxis motivation:

> [O]nce truth is admitted to our conceptual scheme, it cannot be ignored. If determinism is true, it is worthy to be believed. Once a man is allowed to adopt the objective attitude of a spectator, he will seek to see things as they are. . . . [a]nd if that requires him to give up the reactive attitude, he ought to give it up, no matter what the cost in terms of the impoverishment of the texture of human life. (1993, 20)

I think that Lucas's claim is too strong psychologically and is morally debatable. As a matter of psychological fact, we may assign a higher value to non-truth-tracking goals than to maximizing true beliefs, even if we view truth realistically (Double, 1990, 168–69). Normatively, Lucas's recommendation can be disputed in cases where we think that human life would be impoverished by our adopting truth-tracking metaphilosophical scruples. Even if we adopt a realistic conception of truth, we may believe that it is *obligatory* to assign truth-tracking a lower value than other goals that we think are more valuable.

Nonetheless, Lucas's claim nicely illustrates why a philosopher with a strong commitment to Praxis goals will have an incentive to reject a realistic theory of truth. It is easier to place Praxis aims above realistic truth if we already believe that realistic truth does not exist. In addition, the philosopher who holds Praxis goals for philosophy will have an incentive to adopt epistemological views that make realistic truth so hard to obtain that pragmatic considerations in belief fixation would be elevated by contrast. The general theme is: Since we cannot know whether A or *not A* is true by using our intellectual abilities, we must choose using our non-rational abilities.

Tightening up our epistemic standards in order to enhance moral goals is a familiar move. James argues famously in "The Will to Believe" (1897) that because the existence of God can be neither proved nor disproved, we may choose to believe in God. Slightly less famously, James argues in "The Dilemma of Determinism" that "facts practically have hardly anything to do with making us either determinists or indeterminists" and, thus, that we need to cast our vote by appeal to the consequences of the two positions (1962, 152). Kant's critical philosophy can be seen as an embellishment of Humean skepticism to undermine our rational knowledge of reality in order to support the use of faith by default. In *The Vocation of Man,* Fichte (1956) uses Cartesian skepticism to argue that only through the postulation of moral duty can we escape solipsism. Berkeley claims that a moral advantage of his phenomenalist worldview is that it requires the postulation of God to account for the consistency of our sense experience. Much of Rorty's recent writing takes the form: Traditional philosophical questions cannot be answered. So let's ignore them and concentrate on making the world safe for liberalism.

4. The Importance of Having a Metaphilosophy

Anyone who has been around philosophy a short time will recognize the situation where two philosophers reach a point where neither can budge the other with any reason. I find these cases amusing because philosophers, in the Socratic tradition at least, are supposed to be infinitely open to new considerations from any conceivable source. Nonetheless, the dialectic often shuts down entirely. When I was in graduate school, James Cornman recounted a many-articled debate with Wilfrid Sellars on the philosophy of mind/theory of perception in which Cornman advocated eliminating through an adverbial maneuver Sellars's beloved sensa. According to Cornman, after many ripostes by each side, he finally had Sellars pushed into a corner. Sellars replied: "The postulation of sensa is what is distinctive of *my* view!"

I do not know whether this really happened the way Cornman described it, but human nature being what it is, it could have happened. In terms of sheer numbers, ego-defensiveness may explain more human actions than any other explanatory construct, including the needs for food, sex, and safety. Metaphilosophies provide additional resources for defending our views (and our egos) besides simply inflecting the personal pronoun.

If you ask me why I think philosophy should give no favored status to commonsense beliefs (an intermediate principle that does serious damage to moral and free will realism, to say nothing of its bearing on the mind/body problem, personal identity, and the nature of the external world), I do not have to say simply that this is *my view*. Instead I can say, more or less ponderously, *that's what philosophy is*, the imperious inquisitor of all beliefs. If you ask a compatibilist why we should use reflective equilibrium as a means for telling when we are morally responsible and when we are not, rather than question the whole commonsense framework as incompatibilists do, the compatibilist can say either: (1) "Common sense is usually correct about such matters," a factual claim with no special credibility, or (2) "Philosophy is not *in the business* of repudiating common sense," a metaphilosophical claim that is invulnerable to refutation. As I argue in this book, because metaphilosophies are unprovable, citing a metaphilosophy does not settle anything. Nonetheless, citing a metaphilosophy is useful psychologically because it allows us to feel less dogmatic when we are faced with stubborn opposition. It is also useful philosophically, because it allows us to appeal to the coherence of our metaphilosophy, intermediate philosophical principles, and lower-level theories, giving our view a degree of holistic support.

5. The Unprovability of Metaphilosophy: Two Reasons

Metaphilosophies are determined by: (1) our beliefs about what philosophy is, (2) our beliefs about what philosophy can accomplish, and (3) our desires-for-philosophy. Difficulties concerning all three make improbable the attempt to show that any metaphilosophy is best. Given the plurality of conceptions of philosophy noted above, I doubt that we can answer the question of what philosophy *is*, except in some trivial way (e.g., "what persons who are called *philosophers* do that gets them called *philosophers*"). The question of what philosophy can accomplish inherits the problem faced by the former question and adds one of its own. There has always been dispute over whether philosophy can track truths; until we settle that question, it is unlikely that we can decide what philosophy *can* accomplish. The most serious problem for establishing that one metaphilosophy is best, however, arises over the third issue, our desires-for-philosophy.

There can be no deep fact about which desires-for-philosophy are *true*, inasmuch as desires logically are not the sort of psychological states that can be true or false. Using John Searle's terminology, desires have a world-to-mind direction of fit, while truth-tracking psychological states such as beliefs have a mind-to-world direction of fit (1983, 7–9). Some desires, of course, and even some desires-for-philosophy are more widely shared than others, but this is irrelevant to the logical problem that desires cannot correspond to some external condition that would make them true. Because desires per se cannot be true or false, our desires-for-philosophy cannot be true or false. This alone seems to show that no metaphilosophy can be true, with the previous two difficulties adding to the conclusion.

A fall-back position concerning my first point is epistemic. Even if there *could* be some deep metaphysical truth about which desires are true—and I cannot fathom what that would be like—there is no likelihood that we could ever know what that truth is. The reason is the epistemic underdetermination of values by facts: we could never know that we have found the true desires, because having such knowledge entails knowing which desires are objectively best, and in 2,500 years of Western philosophy, no one has ever shown how we can have knowledge of evaluative facts. This would guarantee that as a matter of fact, the selection of a 'true' metaphilosophy cannot be expected. So even if desires could be true, our hopes for knowing that we have hit upon the correct ones cannot be satisfied.

There is a complication worth noting. It may be objected that although *desires* are neither true nor false, *our having certain desires* may be *better* or *worse*—and, by extrapolation, that this is all it takes to make some desires-for-philosophy better or worse than others. (I owe this point to Mark Bernstein.) I reply that I do not understand what it means to say that having certain desires is better than having others except to say either: (i) Certain desires cohere more readily with our other values and goals (the relativistic reading) or (ii) certain desires are absolutely better, or, in Robert Kane's 1994B terminology, are worthwhile from all perspectives (the objective reading).

If the objector says that having certain desires is better than having other desires in the relativistic sense, my argument is not damaged. As long as the objector is talking about relative value, I can reply that among desires in general and desires-for-philosophy in particular there are countless ones that cohere with *someone's* values and goals. Mere relative value does not give the objector a way to resist my claim that if desires cannot be true or false, then the having of one cannot be objectively better than the having of any other.

The objector must mean, therefore, that the having of certain desires is better in the absolute sense. To defend this claim, in turn, requires defending the objectivity of value—that is, that the having of certain desires is better from all perspectives than the having of others. The possibility of such an objective position is often assumed but has never been proven. At this point the metaphilosophical dialectic looms. *If* we assume the objectivity of value, then we will not be barred from saying that the having of certain desires is objectively worthwhile (although we might, I hope, be bothered by the problem of knowing which is worthwhile). This objectivity assumption can be justified metaphilosophically by appeal to Praxis, Underpinnings, or even Conversation views. At the same time, the objectivity of value can be shown to be gratuitous on truth-tracking grounds—that is, on a pure version of Philosophy as Continuous with Science—or so I argue in part II. So if we do not assume the objectivity of value, we must accept my argument that no desires-for-philosophy are more worthwhile than any others.

The upshot of the discussion over my first reason for believing that metaphilosophies are unprovable is this. My argument requires support from the meta-ethical subjectivist position I hold, which in turn requires metaphilosophical support. My argument will be damaged otherwise. For if there could be objective values (and if we could somehow find out what they are), then in principle we could defend having some desire-for-philosophy as objectively better than the rest, and this would support our selecting a certain metaphilosophy. On the other hand, if we accept my metaphilosophy and my claim that it supports the subjectivity of value, we are logically committed to my claims about the unprovability of metaphilosophy, given that the provability of metaphilosophy requires objective values. This reveals again the irony inherent in my central thesis: Given the limitations of philosophical reasoning, I cannot *prove* claims that I think are most likely to be true, including my claim about the unprovability of metaphilosophies.

My second reason for thinking that metaphilosophies are not provable is an inductive one: How could we hope to settle disagreements between familiar disputants about the proper role of philosophy? Consider the "Will to Believe" dispute. W. K. Clifford (1877) and Bertrand Russell (1966) viewed the avoidance of unwarranted beliefs as a *moral* obligation. In my terms, they saw philosophy's role as Worldview Construction and adopted the concomitant view that we should resist the temptation to trade the truth-tracking abilities of the intellect for any amount of psychological benefits. William James (1897) thought that if the answer to a question is neither provable nor disprovable, we ought to choose the option that is most valuable to us as *persons* when the choice is *live*, *momentous*, and *forced*. This shows a Praxis motivation, although James does not exemplify pure Praxis. If he did, he would not have included the various qualifications but would have recommended complete license.

Between Clifford's and Russell's strategy of avoiding false beliefs at all costs and James's willingness to risk having a false belief for a chance at gaining a valuable true one, there are infinitely many intermediate strategies depending on the benefits and costs that we assign to having true and false beliefs. For instance, we might count the value of two true beliefs as equal to the disvalue of one false belief and so on. The position among these that seems best to us will be dictated by what we think philosophy is for, and I see no reason to think that an answer will be forthcoming.

Another example of a fundamental metaphilosophical disagreement occurs over the question of what sort of evidence we need in order to believe in moral truth. J. L. Mackie (1977, chapter 1) demands that moral properties be plausibly located somewhere in the cosmos outside of the positive and negative feelings and attitudes we have about human conduct. Failing to see how that can be done, Mackie draws the non-realist conclusion that moral claims are false. New Wave Moral Realists (Horgan and Timmons's 1993 term) such as Richard Boyd (1988), David Brink (1989), and John Campbell and Robert Pargetter (1986) accept Mackie's challenge and respond by applying the technical resources of analytic philosophy to show how moral properties can be natural properties.

Hilary Putnam, on the other side, believes that the demand for an external 'location' for moral properties is misguided and that the justification of the objectivity of moral truth is easy to find:

> [M]y answer is not that I have some grand metaphysical theory of the essential nature of normativity. . . . The fundamental reason that I myself stick to the idea that there are right and wrong moral judgments . . . is not a metaphysical one. The reason is simply that is the way that we—and I include myself in this "we"—talk and think, and also the way that we are going to go on talking and thinking. (1992, 135)

In this passage Putnam exemplifies Philosophy as Providing Underpinnings for Common Sense and Praxis motivations.

I invite the reader to consider other examples of basic metaphilosophical disputes where there is no reason to think that any side could be shown to be correct. This will provide more reason to believe that metaphilosophical disputes are not resolvable. As to *why* these disputes cannot be resolved, I have already given my own explanation the desire-driven nature of metaphilosophies—earlier in this section.

6. Three Objections to the Relativity of Metaphilosophies

I would like to anticipate three criticisms of my claim that no metaphilosophy is objectively best and that, therefore, metaphilosophical disagreements cannot be resolved. First, a critic might say that there *is* a proper role of philosophy over and beyond the desires-for-philosophy held by individual philosophers. In presenting my view to philosophical audiences, I have heard the following candidates for vindicating a particular metaphilosophy: "Relative to the historical mission of philosophy, such and such is its proper goal" and "Relative to what philosophy is about, such and such is its proper goal." The problem with this sort of proposal is that there have been (and even if there had *not* been, there *could* have been) countless missions pursued by philosophers and countless conceptions of philosophy. What we think the 'true' historical mission of philosophy is depends on our judgment of what writings and movements in the history of philosophy were worthwhile. There is no way to choose a 'correct' metaphilosophical view except by appeal to what we would like to see philosophy accomplish. Until the objector performs the logically impossible task of arriving at 'the correct' metaphilosophy without presupposing such desires, this objection stands at risk from my subjectivist claim that desires cannot be shown to be objectively more worthwhile than others.

A second objection is to offer hybrid metaphilosophies motivated by considerations from several metaphilosophies. Why not say that the proper role of philosophy is to improve the human condition (Philosophy as Praxis) *by* tracking truth (Philosophy as Worldview Construction)? As one of the anonymous readers of this volume points out, this is a plausible interpretation of James and Dewey. Just as we enhance our technologies and the potential for serving moral purposes by our development of truth-tracking science, so philosophy can both track truth and improve the human condition. The true, the good, and the beautiful all converge 'in the end.'

I have emphasized that multiple metaphilosophical motivations are the rule, given that we typically want to accomplish various things by philosophizing. All I need to do to rebut the hybrid objection, though, is to point out that different motivations are not always compatible. For example, recent psychological research on personality shows that self-serving epistemic strategies (e.g., overestimating our efficacy, likability, or intelligence) enhance our motivation, persistence, and, ultimately, happiness, at the expense of truth (Double, 1988B). There may be *socially* beneficial strategies such as the denial of true, but unflattering, statistical data about various disadvantaged groups where Praxis and truth-tracking clash. In setting our goal for philosophy, we decide which motivation shall receive priority *in those cases where conflicts arise.* The question remains, when there is a conflict between Praxis and Worldview Construction motivations (as there is in the free will problem), which shall prevail? To respond that we have a hybrid metaphilosophy that covers all cases would be an implausible evasion of the difficult cases, which are exactly the cases where we need a metaphilosophy to supply direction. Because a hybrid metaphilosophy cannot provide answers for the difficult cases, it becomes just one more candidate among many. If *one* non-truth-valued desire-for-philosophy cannot provide the 'true' metaphilosophy, it would seem very odd arithmetic to conclude that *two or more* non-truth-valued desires can do the trick.

A third objection to my relativism tries to dismiss its importance rather than refute it. The critic might say that metaphilosophically driven disputes are not the whole story in philosophical disagreements. There are conflicts between philosophers who share metaphilosophical views: Worldview Construction theorists include nominalists and Platonists, atheists and theists, direct realists and phenomenalists. Conversely, philosophers with different views of philosophy often agree on substantive philosophical theories. For example, one might arrive at theism via any of my four metaphilosophies. The simple response to this point is that although philosophers with different metaphilosophies may agree, they need not. This is enough to defend the importance of my relativity thesis.

7. Conclusion

In this chapter I have described four idealized metaphilosophies, two of which contain important subsets. These different ways of looking at philosophy constitute a menu of motivations that philosophers bring to the free will problem. Our acceptance of various pairs of intermediate-level philosophical principles are also vital once we get into the specifics of the debate. Once we fix our metaphilosophical position and select supporting intermediate principles, our position on free will is largely in place. In the next chapter I discuss the intermediate principles.

3

Intermediate-Level Philosophical Principles

In this chapter I consider a second factor that contributes to the answers we give to philosophical questions: our adoption of certain intermediate-level philosophical principles. These principles have more content than the metaphilosophies, but they are more general than the answers to lower-level questions such as whether free will or moral truth exists. Intermediate principles contribute to, without absolutely dictating, the answers we give to lower-level philosophical questions. While metaphilosophies reflect our overall vision of philosophy, in terms of both our beliefs about philosophy and our desires-for-philosophy, intermediate principles provide the largely unargued-for premises that bridge the gap between metaphilosophies and our answers to philosophical questions. Differences in intermediate principles also account for the differences in substantive views between practitioners with the same metaphilosophical motivation.

In section 1, I list five pairs of intermediate philosophical principles that are particularly relevant to the free will question. In section 2, I argue for the unprovability of intermediate principles. In section 3, I consider the interplay between metaphilosophies and intermediate principles. In section 4, I consider why someone might accept Philosophy as Continuous with Science and the intermediate principles that correspond with it.

1. Five Pairs of Intermediate Principles

Here are five pairs of regulative principles that serve as especially important premises in arguments concerning the free will problem.

40

Skeptical versus Non-Skeptical Epistemic Standards

The first distinction concerns three sorts of beliefs to which philosophers assign different evidential status: (i) the widely held, prephilosophical beliefs of common sense, (ii) our 'intuitions' or reflective judgments concerning what we ought to say about various thought-experiments, and (iii) phenomenological or introspectively based beliefs. The positions we take on these topics determine how revisionistic we think philosophy should be with respect to common sense and whether we believe that philosophy is best done from the first-person perspective or the third-person. Anyone who adopts the skeptical position on (i), (ii), and (iii) is likely to end up with a more naturalistic picture of the world than someone who is non-skeptical regarding all three.

The first category includes such widely held beliefs as the prephilosophical belief that there is an objective difference between right and wrong and the belief in the existence of free choice. The skeptic on this issue denies that commonsense beliefs merit any evidential status simply due to their popularity or antiquity. Thus, the skeptic holds that if the only thing that a commonsense belief has to recommend it is the fact that it is widely believed, we (epistemically) ought to suspend belief. The non-skeptic assigns the beliefs of common sense a default epistemic primacy: these beliefs merit a prima facie credibility simply because they are widely accepted.

The second disagreement between skeptics and non-skeptics concerns the evidential weight we assign to appeals to 'intuition' in considering philosophical questions. Such appeals are ubiquitous, of course, in philosophy in areas such as normative ethics, personal identity, and the analysis of knowledge, as well the free will issue. In the latter, such appeals typically take the form of the question of whether persons would be free and responsible under various imagined situations. Intuitions play a major role in the debates between the compatibilists and incompatibilists. Skeptics regard appeals to intuition with suspicion because they feel that intuitions are biased by the theories we accept, but non-skeptics are willing to treat intuitions as epistemically credible until they are discredited. For many non-skeptics, intuitions serve as decisive trump in the free will debate.

The third type of disputed belief concerns the status philosophers assign to beliefs that enjoy phenomenological support. There are two questions here: (a) How much support does "S *feels* f" provide for "S *is* f"?

(b) How much support does "S *claims to feel* f" provide for "S *feels* f"? (Combined, these questions lead to a third: [c] How much support does "S *claims to feel* f" provide for "S *is* f"?) These questions are important to the free will problem in two guises: How much evidential weight should we accord to our 'feelings' that we can choose otherwise than we do, that we are morally responsible for our actions, or that we merit reactive attitudes for our actions? And how certain is it that we actually feel the way we say we do when we claim that our introspective awareness shows that we *feel* that we are able to choose otherwise or that we are morally responsible for our actions? (The alternative is that in making such reports we may be relying on an implicit folk-psychological theory of free will rather than introspecting a 'feeling.')

There are several sources of the erosion in the epistemic weight accorded to 'phenomenological reports' by twentieth-century philosophers. Philosophical critics of 'immediacy' such as Wilfrid Sellars, W. V. O. Quine, Wittgenstein, Richard Rorty, Paul Feyerabend, and Paul Churchland have contributed to philosophers' general suspicion of the value of taking first-person reports to be accurate either to the way the world is or to the way the world seems to subjects. Philosophers increasingly are becoming aware of the "telling-more-than-you-can-know" phenomenon from recent cognitive psychology. In a famous paper, Richard Nisbett and Timothy Wilson argue that much of what lay persons typically take to be *introspection* is really *attribution*, the telling of plausible-sounding stories that are popularly accepted as explanations of behavior:

> [T]here may be little or no direct introspective access to higher order cognitive processes. Subjects are sometimes (a) unaware of the existence of a stimulus that importantly influenced a response, (b) unaware of the existence of the response, and (c) unaware that the stimulus has affected the response. . . . [W]hen people attempt to report on their cognitive processes, that is, on the process mediating the effects of a stimulus on a response, they do not do so on the basis of any true introspection. Instead, their reports are based on a priori, implicit causal theories, or judgments about the extent to which a particular stimulus is a plausible cause of a given response. (1977, 231)

Although Nisbett and Wilson couch their discussion in terms of the *causes* of behavior, their results cover philosophers' 'reasons-explanations,' such as "I chose to do act A for reason r."

Sometimes the differences between the skeptics and non-skeptics result from disagreements over facts, as when we disagree on whether commonsense beliefs are generally credible. On the debate over whether philosophy can revise prephilosophical beliefs, Mark Johnston thinks that the issue comes down to the question:

> How far is Common Sense . . . committed to anything that is philosophically problematic? The answer one gives to that question must significantly determine one's conception of the point and scope of philosophy, one's views of how far philosophy legitimately can have revisionary aspirations, one's sense of how satisfying a description of our practices can be if that description indeed leaves everything as it is. (1989, 369)

Revisionist thinkers from Parmenides to Berkeley to Stephen Stich have thought that philosophy can trump commonsense beliefs because common sense is simply wrong about many important things. This is denied by philosophers who believe that common sense is generally correct.

Disagreement between skeptics and non-skeptics also emerges from temperamental differences. By renouncing the privileged evidential status of commonsense beliefs, intuitions, or phenomenological beliefs, the skeptic reveals a willingness to approach philosophy without relying on some of the most common foundations of common sense, religion, and philosophy. In the extreme case, this amounts to giving up the quest for certainty, at least regarding empirical truths. Those philosophers who adopt non-skeptical stances evince a fondness for firmer foundations. These differences typically depend on non-factual metaphilosophical motivations—most important, on what the philosophers desire to accomplish by doing philosophy. Philosophers are notoriously skeptical about their opponents' views and non-skeptical about their own. Camus complains that by giving the planetary model of the atom, science "founders in metaphor" (1955, 15) and loses its claim to provide knowledge, thereby, I presume, leaving the field open to Conversation thinkers like Camus to provide philosophical metaphors.

Realist versus Instrumentalist Interpretations of Theories

The second pair of principles concerns what we take ourselves to be doing when we propose philosophical theories. A realist position takes theoretical claims to presuppose that the entities cited by the theory can be fit into an ontological catalog under some category with clear relations to the other entities already admitted to the catalog, whether physical, non-physical, or 'third realm.' On the realist view, when we start talking about X's in our theories, we must be prepared to say whether X's can be known to exist, and, if so, how (Horgan and Timmons, 1993, 116–17). The competing instrumentalist principle denies that theoretical claims involve this. For instrumentalists, to say that X's exist is to say simply that "X" is a useful part of the theoretical language we use to explain some phenomena. The instrumentalist sees the entire language as connecting up with non-linguistic reality but does not require this of each apparently designating term of the theory. The difference between the realist and instrumentalist views of theories is important when we ask what a free will realist is committed to by claiming that free will and moral responsibility exist.

Ontological Conservativism versus Ontological Liberality

The third pair of intermediate philosophical principles involves the ontological liberality we allow ourselves on those times when we *do* see our theories as trying to catalog reality. A liberal principle allows us to let into our picture of what exists *more* than is absolutely needed to account for the other things that we need to let into our ontology. Robert Kane (1996) reflects the Kantian position that our aspirations, hopes, and desires for human well-being have a legitimate role in shaping our picture of reality. Other philosophers, including philosophers of science, count aesthetic considerations as reasonable grounds for including in our worldview entities that are not strictly necessary on other grounds. A conservative principle endorses a stingy, Occam-like/Quinean view of metaphysical theory construction where we grudgingly let entities into our theory of what exists only when absolutely needed to explain *other* entities that we likewise grudgingly let into our picture. Accordingly, aspirations and other evaluative desiderata have no role to play in our construction of a picture of what exists unless they are somehow needed to explain non-aspirative or non-evaluative entities.

The question of whether all areas of philosophy must meet the same standard of proof provides an illustration of the difference between ontological liberality and conservativism. Philosophers as different in their substantive views as the Logical Positivists, W. V. O. Quine, David Armstrong, Gilbert Harman, and J. L. Mackie believe that all areas require the same degree of proof. Whether we consider the existence of physical objects, mental states, dispositional properties, causation, abstract entities, or moral properties, these philosophers believe that common standards must be met. Such thinkers see similarities between problems in different branches of philosophy, as Quine (1960) does in critiquing nonextensional language in physical theory and psychology, and Mackie (1977) and Harman (1977) do with secondary qualities in perception and moral beliefs. Opponents of this uniformity-of-rigor thesis, such as Thomas Nagel (1979, 145) and Hilary Putnam (1992), accept the Aristotelian dictum that one should not ask for greater precision than the case allows.

On reading this discussion in the manuscript, Alfred Mele suggested that the difference in precision that Aristotle allowed moral philosophy and metaphysics comes from Aristotle's different ideas of what each field is *for*. The aim of the former is to help us to become good, while the aim of the latter is to enhance theoretical knowledge. This idea, whether accurate to Aristotle or not, supports my claim that metaphilosophies interact with intermediate principles, although it points to the complicating fact that we may hold different metaphilosophies for different branches of philosophical inquiry. This is what we would expect, given the complexities of human psychology and the philosophical enterprise.

The principles regarding conservativism versus liberality bear on our evaluation of free will theories that postulate empirically questionable entities, such as the persons of agent theory, Cartesian non-empirical egos, or the amplifications of presumed quantum indeterminacies. More important for my subjectivist aim, the conservative principle supports eliminativist arguments concerning free will such as the ones I provide in Double (1991B) and part II of this book. Finally, these principles bear on moral realism, which I show is intimately connected to the free will problem, because much of the argument for moral non-realism lies in an acceptance of Occam's razor.

Strict versus Liberal Requirements on Explanations

The fourth pair of principles involves our views on how closely informative explanations must approximate deductive-nomological explanations. A strict principle endorses the Hempelian view that all adequate explanations either are deductive-nomological or are elliptical for such deductive nomological explanations (Honderich, 1993, chapter 3; Nagel,

1986, 115–16). A less strict principle holds that explanations that are weaker than deductive-nomological explanations are still informative, whether they provide plausible narratives, which are sometimes called "teleological intelligibility" explanations (Ginet, 1989), or cite probabilities less than 0.5 and, hence, do not provide "contrastive" explanations that explain why an event occurred rather than not (Clarke, 1992).

The position we take on this question is connected with the epistemological dispute already broached: Is the world best understood by looking at it "from the inside" or "from the outside"? Nagel (1979; 1986) has argued that philosophical problems are irresolvable because answers that are acceptable when viewed from the objective, third-person perspective fail when viewed from the subjective perspective. W. T. Jones (1992) argues that the deconstructionists and their foes miss each other because the former take the first-person perspective and the latter take the third-person perspective. In a famous debate, William Drey (1957) argues that historians explain historical events only by imaginatively placing themselves in the positions of the historical figures whose actions are explained, while Carl Hempel (1965) argues that historical explanations must be understood as schematic placeholders for deductive-nomological explanations.

Our position on explanation also has a role to play in our decision on whether libertarian-style undetermined choices would be explainable or not. This falls under the general heading of the 'rationality' of libertarian choices: specifically, whether choices could be rational each of the two ways that they might turn out. Traditional determinist critics of libertarianism have complained that undetermined choices would have no causally sufficient reason and thus would be 'unintelligible.' Libertarians such as C. A. Campbell see such strict demands by the determinist as relying on a question-begging idea of what makes choices intelligible: "Repeatedly it is urged against the Libertarian, with a great air of triumph, that on his view he can't say *why* I now decide to rise to duty, or now decide to follow my strongest desire in defiance of duty. Of course he can't. If he could he wouldn't *be* a libertarian. To 'account for' a 'free' act is a contradiction in terms" (1957, lecture 9).

Hume's Principle

The fifth pair of principles concerns the fact/value distinction—in particular, our acceptance or rejection of the Humean claim that non-moral premises cannot entail moral conclusions. Hume's principle maintains that there is an unbridgeable *semantic gap* between factual and evaluative language. I shall argue that without adding epistemological or ontological premises, Hume's principle can be used to argue for the non-realist's claim that there is an unbridgeable *ontological gap*. I have argued in chapter 1 that an important motivation for looking at the free will problem is to decide whether moral responsibility is possible. If this is our motivation, then an acceptance of moral non-realism risks making the free will problem otiose, on the premise that what is true of moral properties in general is true of moral responsibility.

In addition, as I argue in chapter 9, if we accept Hume's principle we should deny that any account of free choice given in factual terms will be adequate to support *moral* responsibility. I also provide an argument using Hume's principle to support my subjectivist version of free will non-realism. On the other side, philosophers who reject Hume's principle are unlikely to adopt moral non-realism and are unlikely to be moved by arguments predicated on a principle they reject.

2. The Unprovability of Intermediate-Level Principles

The most decisive reason I could offer for thinking that intermediate principles are not provable would be that they are incapable of being true or false. No truth or falsity, no proof. One way to press the point would be to emphasize the regulative role that intermediate principles play in philosophical reasoning. If we liken our answers to lower-level questions to mathematical theorems, then the intermediate principles could be compared to the presupposed axioms from which the theorems are derived. (I owe this comparison to Mark Bernstein.) But the analogy is imperfect, because I think that intermediate principles are not axiomatic but are accepted because of their intrinsic appeal *and* the role they play in interacting with metaphilosophical goals and lower-level theories. This *suggests* that they are neither true nor false but does not support it decisively. To make a stronger case, I shall consider the five pairs of principles in turn.

Unless we accept an extreme Platonism of the 'correct' definition of *knowledge*, our choice about whether to accept skeptical or non-skeptical epistemic principles has to be seen as justified by pragmatic rather than truth-tracking considerations. Depending on what we wish to accomplish by our theorizing, we will assign various epistemic principles weights that are appropriate to those aims. It is difficult to see what it could mean to say that skeptical or non-skeptical principles are *true* except to say that they facilitate our aims. In my terms, this is a matter of metaphilosophy. The case seems likewise concerning the second pair of principles: whether we should adopt realist and instrumentalistic interpretations of theories.

When it comes to choosing between the pair of principles dealing with ontological conservativism and liberality, we might try to make the decision on truth-tracking grounds. One procedure would go as follows: (1) Arrive at a metric for distinguishing between conservative and liberal ontological postulations. (2) Select a representative sample of confirmed and disconfirmed theories from the history of the physical and social sciences and perhaps other disciplines such as 'folk physics' and 'folk psychology.' (3) Use the historical 'database' to decide whether conservative or liberal theories tend to be subsequently confirmed. (4) Assume that *subsequently confirmed* supports *true*. (5) If any statistically significant results emerge from the above steps, extrapolate to the conclusion that the winner is a superior truth-tracking intermediate philosophical principle.

Needless to say, this would be a zany procedure. And even if we went through all these steps and arrived at a conclusion, it would show not that the *principles* endorsing ontological sparseness or liberality are true or false but only that following them provides *better methods for arriving at true theories*—not a very subtle distinction. In practice, our interest in formulating true theories is in constant competition with other motives provided by the Conversation, Praxis, and Underpinnings metaphilosophies. This being so, our decisions on ontological sparseness or liberality are going to be made on motivational grounds, even if one of the postulational stances enjoys a greater history of truth-tracking successes.

The moral given for the first three intermediate principles repeats itself for the question of how far informative explanations can depart from the deductive-nomological model. This leaves Hume's principle as the most likely of the intermediate principles to be a candidate for being true or false. Let us allow that it may be, or at least that it can be understood as true or false once we go through the analytical process of defining what we mean by the key terms *moral, non-moral, entails,* and so on. Even so, our knowledge of its truth or falsity seems unlikely, given that Hume's principle remains in dispute after 250 years and the fact that its connection to morality makes discussion of it less of a purely logical exercise than the discussion of any other issue in the philosophy of language.

In sum, four of the five pairs of intermediate principles seem not to be capable of being truth-valued, and even in the case of the fifth, our acceptance or rejection is going to depend on non-truth-valued factors. For these reasons, our choices among the intermediate principles will be made on the basis of our interests and desires, not on the basis of our ability to discern truths. As with metaphilosophies, our choices are subject not to truth-tracking evidence that one alternative is more reasonable than another but to arguments that appeal to our desires, feelings, and emotions.

3. The Interplay of Metaphilosophies, Intermediate Principles, and Lower-Level Theories

Psychologically speaking, our positions on metaphilosophy, intermediate principles, and lower-level philosophical theories influence our views in the other areas. In terms of justification, also, views at each level can help reinforce views at the others. Because the relationship between the three is naturalness or plausibility of fit, philosophers will tend to hold some combinations and avoid others. Objectively plausible combinations that are not related by logical entailment will correspond to philosophers' acceptances of those combinations, as we would expect on the premise that philosophers are able to recognize what is plausible. As one reader notes, Humean epistemological scruples (an intermediate principle) may support both moral non-realism (a lower-level theory) and naturalism (a higher-level generalization that may be reached via Philosophy as Continuous with Science). The important thing to note is that there is no single top-down or bottom-up structure, either evidentially or in terms of how philosophers think about these issues.

In the last chapter I argued that metaphilosophies cannot *be shown* to be better than others, and that on subjectivism it is impossible for one metaphilosophy to *be* better than another. Either way, our choice of a metaphilosophy depends on our wills rather than some objective fact outside of us. Metaphilosophies support our intermediate principles by providing aims for the intermediate principles to serve, such as aesthetic considerations, praxis, underpinning some other area of thought, or truth-tracking. Our intermediate principles, which also are not provable as true or false, are largely evaluated in terms of their contribution to our other philosophical and metaphilosophical aims. The specific answers to philosophical problems we decide to accept, which may be true or false, inherit the willful character of the metaphilosophies and intermediate principles with which they are connected.

Philosophers are ingenious enough to put together combinations that would astonish the lay person. Thus, any attempt to create a truly exhaustive listing of combinations of metaphilosophies, intermediate principles, and lower-level theories would be chimerical. Nonetheless, there are some notable connections. Consider first the difference in the way that philosophers motivated by Praxis and Worldview Construction considerations would think about the first intermediate principle. Praxis metaphilosophy requires flexibility regarding its position on whether to accept skeptical vs. anti-epistemic standards, given that Praxis is motivated by the desire to make philosophy serve human well-being. Praxis thinkers may decide that these goals are served by endorsing an epistemic position that gives prima facie warrant to the beliefs of common sense, reflective intuitive judgments, or first-person experience. But when Praxis aims seem stifled by common sense, intuitions, or phenomenological beliefs—when these beliefs play a 'reactionary' role relative to the aims of Praxis—then Praxis thinkers require the latitude to become radical and refuse to accord those beliefs special warrant. It all depends on the specifics of the problem at hand when the Praxis thinker considers the problem, which is to say that Praxis motivation is, to use Rorty's term, *historicist*.

If we adopt Philosophy as Continuous with Science, which places truth-seeking above all else irrespective of how those truths affect what Ted Honderich calls our *life hopes* (1988; 1993) or moral behavior, then the above degree of flexibility will seem indefensible. Instead, our selection of epistemic principles will need to be made by asking which epistemic principles are most likely to give a truthful account of the world. This is not to suggest that all philosophers who are moved by this metaphilosophy will adopt skeptical epistemic principles. Some may endorse foundationalism or the prima facie acceptability of commonsense views. Others may think that a flamboyant exercise of inference to the best explanation is apt to provide an accurate worldview. We could even think that there *is* no one best overall epistemic strategy. Perhaps *both* skeptics and non-skeptics should ply their trades, just as the exercise of a plurality of concepts of rationality might contribute more to the collective rationality of intellectual exploration than adherence to just one (Stich, 1990, chapter 6). But in each of these cases, those who adopt Philosophy as Continuous with Science make their decisions about skepticism on the basis of whether skepticism serves the interests of their metaphilosophy, not on the basis of extra-truth-seeking interests.

Second, consider the intermediate principles concerning ontological liberality. Philosophy as Conversation and Philosophy as Praxis motivations appear to support ontological liberality more readily than Philosophy as Underpinnings and Philosophy as Worldview Construction motivations do, because the former metaphilosophies renounce the aim of truth-tracking. This is not to deny that Underpinnings and Worldview Construction also sometimes contribute to a bloated ontology when doing so is deemed necessary to perform the tasks of philosophy they recognize. The postulation of numbers, universals, possible worlds, nonphysical minds, and a transcendent God have been proposed in the name of underpinning common sense, religion, and science, as well as for the purpose of completing an accurate philosophical picture of the world.

A third illustration of the interplay between metaphilosophies, intermediate principles, and lower-level theories lies in the difference between the two varieties of Worldview Construction: Philosophy as Continuous with Science and Philosophy as Non-Continuous with Science. Both varieties endorse the aim of truth-tracking as philosophy's highest goal, but differences at the level of intermediate principles tend to produce differences in lower-level theories.

Consider Philosophy as Continuous with Science. Suppose we flesh out the Worldview metaphilosophy by endorsing the following intermediate principles: a skepticism toward the beliefs of common sense, intuitions, and first-person phenomenological experience along with an endorsement of inference to the best explanation; a realist interpretation of theories; stingy scruples regarding ontological postulations; rigid demands for informative explanations; and acceptance of Hume's principle. Armed with this ammunition, it would be easy to reach a naturalistic picture of things: materialism in the mind/body problem, atheism, scientific realism as an account of the nature of the physical world, and moral non-realism in meta-ethics. Traditional epistemology would be replaced with logic, scientific method, and attempts to improve our cognitive strategies through the study of how we reason. Value theory would become naturalized by examining the psychological bases that lead us to make the judgments we do about values. Most important for this book, a similar minimizing approach would be taken toward free will and moral responsibility, as *free* and *moral* were taken to be honorific, non-designating terms. As noted above, a naturalistic worldview is the likely result of the application of the intermediate principles that distinguish Philosophy as Continuous with Science from Philosophy as Non-Continuous with Science.

Some Worldview Construction theorists reject the stringent intermediate principles that go into Philosophy as Continuous with Science, thereby falling into my catch-all category Philosophy as Non-Continuous with Science. Because the decision to adopt intermediate principles is a case of practical reasoning, both belief and desire can contribute to the result. Consider belief first. Worldview thinkers might reject the harsh intermediate principles of Philosophy as Continuous with Science because they believe that other principles will produce a more accurate worldview. Such thinkers might have different ideas of how good science proceeds. More radically, philosophers moved by the truth-tracking motivation of Philosophy as Worldview Construction might endorse *any* epistemic principles. Such theorists could believe, for instance, that the best way to construct an accurate picture of reality is to rely on revelation from God and that the word of God can be faultlessly ascertained by carefully listening to voices in our heads or by reading religious texts. Or they might think, as many non-philosophers do, that lots of religious and common-sense beliefs are simply self-authenticating ("If you have to ask what makes them true, you'll never know").

The point that our choice of epistemic principles is not determined by our metaphilosophical motivation applies to the other intermediate principles as well. Theorists who endorse Worldview Construction may adopt any position they want regarding instrumentalism, ontological liberality, explanations, or Hume's principle. It is, therefore, easy to see why Worldview Construction has to be divided between practitioners who see philosophy as continuous with science in my stipulated sense and those who do not, even if we ignore the history of philosophy, which gives ample evidence of the distinction.

Differences between Philosophy as Continuous with Science and Philosophy as Non-Continuous with Science can be traced to different desires as well as different beliefs. Philosophers moved by Philosophy as Non-Continuous with Science, although desiring to construct an accurate picture of things, may be motivated by the Praxis aim to provide for human well-being as well. This desire was at the root of Plato's fascination with the form of The Good and Kant's willingness to entertain the existence of God, the soul, and libertarian freedom in the face of his conviction that these could not be known by reason. Praxis desires may motivate the acceptance of intermediate principles that support Philosophy as

Non-Continuous with Science: ontological liberalism, loose standards of explanation, and a rejection of the fact/value distinction. Likewise, such principles may receive support from other metaphilosophical motivations: the desire to provide interesting philosophical conversation or the desire to underpin common sense or religion.

4. Why Adopt Philosophy as Continuous with Science?

It is fair to ask why anyone would or should adopt Philosophy as Continuous with Science and the intermediate principles that go with it, given that this view contributes to philosophical conclusions that many thinkers find unappealing. According to the all-things-considered approach mentioned in chapter 1, the unattractiveness of the philosophical conclusion is a relevant factor in our choice of how we think we should approach philosophy.

Regarding the psychological question "Why would anyone want to adopt Philosophy as Continuous with Science?," I doubt that anyone has a scientifically reputable answer. Alvin Goldman and Stephen Stich inform me in correspondence that they know of no psychological research on why philosophers philosophize the way they do. If we dare to address this question, it must be done speculatively. As a philosopher, I find this topic extremely interesting, even if my hypotheses are just speculation. With that qualification, let me suggest some reasons why Philosophy as Continuous with Science might in fact appeal to philosophers and some reasons why Philosophy as Continuous with Science is a plausible metaphilosophy. In this way, my suggestions address both the psychological question of why philosophers *would* adopt this view and the normative question of why they *should*.

Part of my answer has already been broached—namely, the holistic relationship between metaphilosophies, intermediate principles, and lower-level philosophical solutions. Because views at all levels influence those at the others, we might be motivated to accept a higher-level view because we like some of the lower-level theories that correspond to it. For instance, our prior acceptance of atheism might support our belief in ontological parsimony or Philosophy as Continuous with Science as readily as the latter two might influence our acceptance of the former.

Another part of my answer has to do with the vision of the philosopher as the courageous truth-seeker who faces the direst of facts with Stoic

detachment. (For me, the persona of W. K. Clifford I derived from reading "The Ethics of Belief" was very moving, although I think Clifford's
argument is hyperbolic and philosophically weak.) Those of us who like
Philosophy as Continuous with Science can build a heroic vision of that
metaphilosophy that is very ego-gratifying. In addition, one must not
underestimate the titillation and ego-boost we receive from shocking
lay persons and other philosophers with our uncommonsensical views,
especially when we claim that whole areas of philosophy that others hold
dear are based on confusions.

I can offer a less cynical gloss on the thought that Philosophy as
Continuous with Science is admirable because of its courageous, non-
conformist commitment to truth-tracking. Non-truth-tracking metaphilosophies tacitly presuppose that some area of human inquiry tracks truth.
Even Praxis thinkers, who do not set truth-tracking to be their highest
philosophical goal, need accurate information. Conversation thinkers
assume that some statements are true, despite the fact that they disparage Truth. Underpinnings thinkers, by definition, think truth can be found
in areas other than philosophy. Thus, for the other metaphilosophies, if
philosophy does not provide truth, then common sense, science, religion,
or some other area must be assumed to do so. But what reason, other than
dogmatism, would suggest that these areas are better able to perform the
feat than philosophy?

Division of labor becomes relevant. I am reminded of Richard Rorty's
claim that it is good for the society that *some* group of nit-picking spe-
cialists (analytic philosophers) be highly skilled in pulling apart arguments. By analogy we might reason that it is good for the society that
some group of cold-blooded theoreticians (philosophers motivated by
Philosophy as Continuous with Science) devote their energies solely to
the business of truth-tracking at the most general level. Such thinkers
would 'follow the argument' wherever it leads, even if the destination is
not one we like. This would be similar to having experts solely devoted
to giving us accurate information—whether we like it or not—upon which
to make our policy decisions involving global warming, overpopulation,
and the hazards of nuclear waste.

If we temper our commitment to truth-tracking in order to accommodate Praxis or Underpinnings or Conversation goals, then unless the world
is very strange, we are less likely to produce philosophical theories with
the best chance of being true. A disturbing question to ask students when

examining the traditional arguments for God's existence is whether they would find the arguments compelling if they did not think that there is a payoff for them if God exists. If we are influenced by these other meta-philosophical motivations, we are like trial judges who not only let their moral attitudes about punishment influence them when sentencing but also allow those feelings to bias what evidence they allow to be heard on the question of whether the accused committed the crime. This is not necessarily (from an all-things-considered point of view) undesirable in every imaginable case, but usually it would be. It would make for bad truth-tracking *and* bad practice, because practice requires accurate information.

These sorts of considerations may not be psychologically powerful to many philosophers. Nor are they logically impeccable, relying as they do on disputable analogies. I do not find them entirely negligible, however. Thus, I end up where I think I should when it comes to supporting Philosophy as Continuous with Science. This sort of inconclusive reason is the most that supporters of this metaphilosophy can say to support their views that would be consistent with their own tenets. Compare: We cannot consistently claim to know that we have no knowledge. We cannot consistently claim to prove that Philosophy as Continuous with Science is correct, if that metaphilosophy holds that metaphilosophies cannot be proven and cannot be true.

5. Conclusion

In this chapter I sketched five pairs of intermediate-level philosophical principles that are relevant to debates over free will. These principles, along with the four metaphilosophies, serve as the unargued-for premises that separate thinkers on specific debates over free will. Because metaphilosophies and the intermediate principles cannot be shown to be best, and because our answers to free will questions depend on them, no adjudication of those questions is possible. In the next two chapters I provide ten cases to show how meta-level considerations are crucial to the free will debate.

4

How the Free Will Debate Depends on Metaphilosophy (I)

In this chapter I provide five illustrations of how our metaphilosophies and intermediate-level philosophical principles produce different answers in debates over free choice. Specific positions on these debates are plausible if and only if we adopt supporting meta-level views. But I argued in the last two chapters that no metaphilosophy or intermediate principle can be shown to be more reasonable than its competitors. We are forced to admit, therefore, that the most we can do is relativize our answers to our metaphilosophies and intermediate principles, but we cannot show anyone with different meta-level views that the answers we prefer are best.

The issues that I examine are: (1) Reasons for believing in free will. (2) Who bears the burden of proof in showing that free will exists? (3) How inventive may philosophers be in trying to accommodate free will? (4) An examination of Peter Strawson's justification of blame. (5) The debate over whether libertarianism allows for satisfactory explanations of libertarian choices.

1. Reasons for Believing in Free Will

A familiar route to libertarianism and compatibilism is to assert that freedom exists and then argue that the *other* accounts of it are less plausible than yours. Susan Wolf argues for her brand of compatibilism by asserting that free will exists and by rejecting libertarianism (1990, 55–56) and other compatibilist competitors (1990, chapter 2). Ira Singer (1993) accepts compatibilism because "libertarianism is false, leaving some variety of compatibilism as our only hope of rescuing meaningful talk of freedom." The compatibilist reasoning of Wolf and Singer has the form:

1. Either libertarianism or compatibilism is true.
2. Libertarianism is false.
3. Therefore, (some variety of) compatibilism is true.

On the other side, libertarians are moved to endorse metaphysical indeterminacy with its notorious difficulties because they are convinced that only indeterminism will make possible the freedom they believe we have. Their reasoning looks like this:

1. Either libertarianism or compatibilism is true.
2. Compatibilism is false.
3. Therefore, (some variety of) libertarianism is true.

It is natural to ask both groups why they believe that the first premise is true. To this question, a standard reply is that it follows from the two premises "If free will exists, then either libertarianism or compatibilism is true" and "Free will exists." The question now becomes, why believe that free will exists?

One might expect from someone motivated by Philosophy as Worldview Construction unaffected by the pull of the other metaphilosophies a fallibilistic expression of belief in free choice. As has been widely noted, the freedom of our choices is not one of the introspectably obvious constituents of the world, even if we adopt the non-skeptical view that introspective beliefs about the way the world *seems* yields evidence about the way the world *is*. Hard determinists, for example, think such feelings of freedom are entirely worthless. It is not even true that our first-person 'experience of' freedom compels us to *believe* we are free if we are careful epistemically (Double, 1991A). Moreover, unlike the concept *choice*, *free choice* serves a theoretical role not in explaining human behavior but only in evaluating it. So the epistemic credentials of free will are pretty flimsy. But those who adopt either of the above arguments for the reality of free choice typically treat free choice not as simply one more component of their theoretical vision of the cosmos, but rather as something they are quite *sure* exists. This degree of conviction needs an explanation.

At this point the role of metaphilosophy is illuminating. If we use the belief in free choice as a premise to argue that libertarianism or compatibilism must be correct, as with the two arguments above, then that belief logically cannot be justified by our theoretical acceptance of either theory. We could claim to justify libertarianism or compatibilism by our acceptance of free choice and justify our belief in free choice by our acceptance of libertarianism or compatibilism, and try to claim such circular reasoning as a virtue. But this would be to admit that neither the belief in free choice nor our free will theory is justified. Instead, if it is to be justified at all, our belief in free choice must be justified on grounds other than by our acceptance of a theory that is to be justified on the supposition of free will.

One venerable way to try to obviate this difficulty is to claim that we have strong introspective evidence not just for free will in my sense of choices that support moral responsibility but also for libertarian free will. The libertarian C. A. Campbell claims that even if there were overwhelming reasons for believing in determinism, the introspectible feeling that we make indeterminate choices has just as strong epistemic credentials as *all* of the theoretical reasons for believing in determinism combined: "There is no reason whatever why a belief that we find ourselves obliged to hold *qua* practical beings should be required to give way before a belief we find ourselves obliged to hold *qua* theoretical beings" (1957, 170). But determinists and indeterminists alike have wisely rejected the appeal to introspection, because undetermined choice (as opposed to our lack of recognition of causes for our choices) is not introspectible at all.

A more subtle move to justify the existence of free choice comes from van Inwagen (1983, 206–9), who claims that we *know* that we are morally responsible for our behavior and that we may infer that we possess whatever sort of freedom that moral responsibility entails. Randolph Clarke uses a similar premise in sketching his argument for agent causation: "(1) We are morally responsible agents; (2) If we are morally responsible agents, then we act with free will; (3) If we act with free will, then determinism is false; (4) If determinism is false and still we act with free will, then we agent-cause our actions" (1993, 200).

On this strategy, our feelings of guilt, pride, and recrimination are taken to establish that we are morally responsible for the actions that arouse those feelings. This strategy is less questionable than the view that we can introspect indeterminacy, because it does not claim that we can observe the lack of causes. This tack relies instead on the premise that moral responsibility presupposes free choice in *some* form, whether libertarian or compatibilist. Whether moral responsibility requires the *sort* of free choice that the libertarians or compatibilists propose, in turn, is addressed by substantive philosophical argument.

Against this strategy, however, we must ask whether our 'feelings' of moral responsibility are any more evidence for moral responsibility than our introspective unawareness of determinism is evidence that our choices are undetermined. Why not see our feelings of moral responsibility simply as psychological data in need of a theoretical explanation with no preemptive epistemic credentials? Once we take this approach, it may turn out that our feelings of moral responsibility are better explained by appealing to psychological facts about us and our moral training, rather than by seeing them as reliable indicators of the real property of moral responsibility that we discern. This approach, of course, is an application of the moral non-realist treatment of our moral intuitions in general. If we consider this possibility, this particular argument for moral responsibility will be stalled, because we will recognize that the argument depends on the successful outcome of a perennial, unresolvable meta-ethical debate. So the claim that we 'just know' that we are morally responsible needs substantial assistance before it can be taken seriously. Metaphilosophy can provide such assistance.

I can think of three ways to supplement the argument for moral responsibility, each using a different meta-level principle. (As noted, we can combine metaphilosophical motivations.) The first involves what we think of the epistemic warrant of introspection in general. As I just noted, so long as we treat our introspective belief in moral responsibility as raw data to be interpreted in the best theoretical way, that belief will not be credible. A simple maneuver by the realist would be to *legislate* that introspective data is not mere data in need of explanation but has a privileged epistemic status that places the burden of proof on the non-realist (see Nagel, 1986, 143, on the prima facie epistemic status of moral realism). This can be done by relying on one of the non-skeptical intermediate principles from chapter 3. The principle that assigns prephilosophical beliefs special status is consistent with several metaphilosophies.

A second way to support the claim that we know that we are morally responsible is not by assigning a special *epistemic* status to introspective beliefs but by making a frank appeal to the *moral* importance of our belief in moral responsibility. Howard Kahane summarizes the moral motivation for accepting free will this way: "[L]ying behind [our] refutation is a very strong desire to hold people accountable for their actions and choices, and a very strong need to admire and reward those who sacrifice for their duty and to hate and to punish the devil's work. And that, ultimately, is the basic reason for rejecting hard determinism" (1983, 46–47).

If we think that in philosophy moral desiderata can trump truth-tracking considerations, then adopting the skeptical view that sees our belief in moral responsibility as raw data in need of an explanation may seem unacceptable. Instead, clear intuitions regarding praiseworthiness and blameworthiness *morally* would have to be counted among the foundations of our moral thinking. As G. E. Moore said about knowledge, if we cannot agree that we know that this is a hand, we won't get anywhere in epistemology. By analogy, philosophy cannot serve moral purposes if it treats the clearest paradigms of moral knowledge as having no preemptive evidential worth. The moral argument that we know that we are morally responsible derives from Philosophy as Praxis considerations.

A third way to support the claim that we know that we are morally responsible is by emphasizing the important part that our belief in moral responsibility plays in "the fabric of common sense." We might emphasize, as Peter Strawson (1962) does, that we reveal our belief in moral responsibility by our practices and by those reactive attitudes that are characteristic of the way we look at other persons. For Strawson, it makes no sense to ask whether we *should* give up ways of thinking and acting that we *cannot* relinquish (1962, 74). Philosophy's job is to explicate commonsense views, not to undermine them. This approach reflects the metaphilosophy of Philosophy as Providing Underpinnings for Common Sense.

2. The Burden-of-Proof Issue

Is the burden of proof on those who deny that free will exists or on those who affirm free choice? W. V. O. Quine (1960, chapter 1) thinks that every item in our 'catalog' of the world beyond our sensory stimulations is a posit that must be justified theoretically in terms of its ability to help explain things already admitted to the catalog. Quine's view seems to me to entail that: (i) the existence of choices needs to be theoretically justified as a posit that we need to make in order to understand human behavior, and (ii) the distinction between free and unfree choices needs to be justified. Thus, it seems to me that on a Quinean 'everything-is-a-posit' view of ontology, free choices need theoretical justification no less than the esoteric entities of physics or the macroscopic physical objects of common sense. Wilfrid Sellars also sees the burden of proof to lie with the free will realist. Granted that freedom is part of our Manifest Image of Man-in-the-World, Sellars asks whether we can legitimize it by integrating it into our Scientific Image of Man-in-the-World (1963, chapter 1, 38–40).

Against this approach, Antony Flew maintains that the fact that we have *paradigms* of free choice cinches the case that free will exists:

> [T]o say that a person could have helped doing something is not to say that what he did was in principle unpredictable nor that there were no causes anywhere which determined that he would as a matter of fact act in this way. It is to say that *if* he had chosen to do otherwise, he would have been able to do so; that there were alternatives, within the capacities of one of his physical strength, of his I.Q., with his knowledge, and open to a person in his situation. . . . [T]he meaning of the key phrase 'could have helped it' can be elucidated by looking at simple paradigm cases: such as those in which fastidious language users employ it *when the madness of metaphysics is not upon them.* (1959, 150, my italics)

One way to illustrate the role that different metaphilosophical motivations play in the burden-of-proof dispute is to see how philosophers respond to what I call the *fragmentation problem*. In chapter 7 below, I argue that in its fragmentation and value-ladenness, *free choice* is similar to *jerk*. It is unlikely that philosophers would insist that there exists a class of jerks, that is, a class defined by their sharing an objective characteristic of jerkiness or jerkhood, as opposed to individuals whom some persons dislike at various times for various reasons. This is because of the fragmentary and contradictory nature that such a class would have to have. If we take fragmentation (or fragmentation along with evaluativeness) to count decisively against the existence of jerks, why not do the same thing with free choices? Perhaps it is because we have a *stake* in the objectivity of free choices that we do not have in the objectivity of jerks.

If we accept Philosophy as Worldview Construction and the specific Quinean point that everything we include in our ontology is a posit in need of justification, then the fragmentation argument becomes highly persuasive. Perhaps there *is* an objective and non-contradictory class of free choices to be found and explicated, whether indeterministic or deterministic, or even both, if free will is possible either way. But if the fragmentation is as drastic as I think it is, then on this combination of metaphilosophy and intermediate principle, the existence of free choice is put in jeopardy. The most plausible way to 'locate' free will is to reduce 'it' to our disjointed, subjective thoughts about when we are free and unfree.

On the other hand, if we think that the burden of proof is on the non-realist to demonstrate that free choice does not exist, then the fragmentation argument may appear unpersuasive. At least two metaphilosophies support this view of the burden of proof: Underpinnings and Praxis. If we believe that *the job* of philosophy is to underpin common sense, then the difficulties that impress the advocate of Philosophy as Continuous with Science will seem to indicate that at most more analytical work needs to be done. At worst, these difficulties would be taken to show how philosophers can be bewitched by language (Wittgenstein) or frightened by bugbears (Dennett) into fantastic theories. On this conception of philosophy, philosophy is for underpinning common sense, not undermining it. Perhaps we have to admit that *free* does fragment and that perhaps neither the incompatibilists nor the compatibilists can give the whole story, but this gives us scant reason to scrap the whole concept (Cockburn, 1992, 387). On Philosophy as Praxis, the burden of proof also falls on those who argue against free choice, given the moral importance of freedom. On this view, even if fragmentation points to a *theoretical* problem, such a difficulty does not merit much weight, given the total picture.

3. How Far May Philosophers 'Go' to Accommodate Free Will?

Incompatibilists and compatibilists disagree over whether free choice requires a special structural underpinning in the cosmos—to wit, indeterminism. Robert Kane (1985; 1996) proposes a complex theory, based on the amplification of quantum indeterminacies, that makes many of our choices undetermined, thereby making us the ultimate causes of our actions. Roderick Chisholm (1976), Richard Taylor (1966), Randolph Clarke (1993), and Timothy O'Connor (1995A) propose an even more daring *agent theory* in which we are unmoved movers (or, as Clarke puts it, not totally moved movers) who bring about choices in a different way than occurs in the event causation that we believe governs all non-agent-causal macroscopic phenomena. Hard determinists agree that freedom requires undetermined choices but deny that the cosmos is so structured. Although some hard determinists such as B. F. Skinner (1971) are pleased by the conclusion that we are not free, many express sadness. The latter are like those moral realists who, when they lose their belief in divine commands or Platonic forms, regretfully conclude that morality cannot be sustained.

Now, suppose that we felt that these incompatibilist views represent philosophy at its pretentious worst: that the incompatibilists try to usurp science's domain by making grandiose, a priori pronouncements that could never be known to be true and by generally taking themselves too seriously. Suppose we also thought that the best talents of philosophers lie in their ability to analyze complicated concepts. Someone who held these views about the foibles and merits of philosophers would be likely to take an opposing view on what philosophers may 'do' regarding the free will problem. Their advice would be to quit speculating in pseudo-science, as the libertarians do, and quit drawing portentous conclusions from negative answers to pseudo-scientific speculations, as the hard determinists do. Instead, philosophers should provide the conceptual analyses needed to help us distinguish between free and unfree choices without metaphysical excesses.

This deflationary view of philosophy supports the conclusion that some variety of compatibilism is the only *methodologically sound* program we can pursue regarding free will. On this metaphilosophy, the serious work for the philosopher lies in the details, and each little bit of 'normal philosophy' that we do brings us closer to putting the free will problem to rest. Although this method-based argument is not the only route to compatibilism, it is a historically influential route. More important, this view provides a rationale that is internally coherent and irrefutable once we accept the metaphilosophy that supports it. This is Philosophy as Underpinnings of Common Sense.

4. Strawson's Subjectivist Account of Blame

Suppose that malefactor M, and not innocent bystander B, wittingly performs some misdeed A. Suppose that, seeing this, we feel a strong negative emotional reaction, followed by the expression of blame, and then by the judgment that punishment is warranted. To receive blame or punishment, *ceteris paribus*, is to be treated worse than not to be blamed or punished. So to express our reactive attitudes toward M, to blame M, or to punish M and not B (and not simply to keep our feelings to ourselves) requires moral justification according to the moral principle that treating one person worse than another is unfair unless there is moral justification for doing so.

Peter Strawson suggests a controversial subjectivist account in his famous "Freedom and Resentment" (1962). According to Strawson, the psychological foundation of our practice of holding persons morally responsible is our tendency to feel personal reactive attitudes such as resentment and gratitude and impersonal or vicarious reactive attitudes such as moral indignation. "[O]ur proneness to reactive attitudes is a natural fact . . . neither calling for nor permitting a general 'rational' justification" (1980, 265). Thus, the appropriateness of having reactive attitudes presupposes no theoretical or metaphysical commitments (e.g., indeterminism). Blame and punishment are "all of a piece with" (1962, 77) our having reactive attitudes, which in turn is part of what it is to view persons as persons. By citing the reactive attitudes, we give the compatibilist "something more to say" (1962, 62) to justify the practice of holding persons responsible than merely citing the beneficial consequences of that practice. So for Strawson, behaviors that express our reactive attitudes are justified in terms of the reactive attitudes, which do not themselves need to be justified.

Strawson's view is subjectivist because he claims that our propensity to have reactive attitudes *constitutes* moral responsibility: Moral responsibility is not a characteristic that exists objectively in those persons we blame over and beyond the reactive attitudes we hold toward them. Gary Watson calls this view 'expressivism':

> In Strawson's view, there is no such independent notion of responsibility that explains the propriety of the reactive attitudes. The explanatory priority is the other way around: It is not that we hold people responsible because they *are* responsible; rather, the idea (*our* idea) that we are responsible is to be understood by the practice, which itself is not a matter of holding some propositions to be true, but of expressing our concerns and demands about our treatment of one another. (1987, 258)

Thus, for Strawson, moral responsibility 'exists' only in the psychological states of blamers rather than in blamees, a classic subjectivist move. As Jonathan Bennett sees it:

My feeling of indignation at what you have done is not a perception of your objective blameworthiness, nor is it demanded of me by such a perception. It expresses my emotional make-up, rather than reflecting my ability to recognize a blame-meriting person when I see one. The gap left by the Schlickian account is not to be filled in by facts about desert or about the meriting of blame[;] . . . rather, in Strawson's words, "it is just these attitudes themselves which fill the gap." (1980, 24)

At this point, let us adopt the viewpoint of a critic of Strawson. According to this critic, the expression of negative reactive attitudes, blame, and punishment require moral justification, because these treatments make persons worse off than they would otherwise be. But the only plausible justification of blame and punishment is the fact that those persons blamed are blameworthy, that they really *are* morally responsible irrespective of anyone's feelings toward them. For this critic, this may not be a sufficient condition for these behaviors, but it is necessary. Because moral responsibility is supposed, inter alia, to justify the differential treatment of malefactors and innocents, it seems to be a moral characteristic that is going to require justification by reference to the person blamed.

Many traditional moral theories sought to establish moral truth by appeal to non-natural entities. In terms of the question regarding M, such theories could be read as saying that M is blameworthy because, for example, M knowingly (or even unknowingly) violated a stricture of God or acted contrary to an intuitable Platonic truth about morality. On such views, M may be blamed because M is blameworthy in the sense that the violation of these rules *makes* M blameworthy. This is a real characteristic of M, no less than M's height and age. In my opinion, such theories provide no enlightening answer to the question of *how* a violation of a theological or secular dictate could *make* one blameworthy; they do not provide a more informative answer than 'it just does.' But at least these views try to make blameworthiness a feature of those who are blamed, something that Strawsonian subjectivism does not attempt.

My critic of Strawson believes that only real blameworthiness as a characteristic of those blamed will justify blame and punishment. Blameworthiness, if it is a fact at all, seems above all a fact about those blamed. But on Strawson's view, blameworthiness is not a characteristic of those blamed, since it is nothing more than the subjective feelings of blamers. Logically, Strawson's (or any subjectivist's) 'relocation' of moral responsibility to the attitudes and feelings of those who hold persons responsible cannot answer the critic's demand for an *objective* justification of the differential treatment of malefactors and innocents.

According to the critic, Strawsonian subjectivism refuses to address this normative question. Even if *having* reactive attitudes does not need a general justification (more on this later), that is irrelevant to the critic's concern. The difficulty is not over the version of the open-question argument that reads "Granted, we naturally tend to feel X, but is X a justifiable way to feel?" The version that causes trouble for Strawson is "Granted, we naturally tend to feel X, but are behaviors that *express X* and *negatively affect persons in doing so* justifiable behaviors?"

If we appeal to a familiar moral intuition, we cannot exempt from the need for moral justification any type of expressive behavior that adversely affects persons. Suppose, for instance, that on a distant planet evolution occurred very differently than it did on Earth, producing a species of humans I call the *Heartless Beings* (Double, 1991B, 184–86), none of whom feel benevolence or sympathy but only malicious sentiments. The naturalness of these feelings to the Heartless Beings goes no way toward justifying the behaviors that stem from them. Thus, it would be confused to say that these *behaviors*, as opposed to *feelings*, neither call for nor permit a general justification. Perhaps feelings are not to be justified but, on that common moral intuition, behaviors should be.

The Strawsonian has a response to this criticism. Perhaps Strawson's critic is being needlessly metaphysical and has taken things too literally. Consider a consequentialist account of moral responsibility that holds that persons are morally responsible for their behavior just in case the practice of holding them responsible is beneficial (see Dennett, 1984, chapter 7, and Schlick, 1939, chapter 7). On this view, there need be no deep, metaphysical fact about those blamed, but only empirical facts about the consequences of holding persons responsible. There are two ways that the consequentialist could argue. An 'eliminativist' strategy would maintain that persons justifiably may be blamed despite the fact that they are not *blameworthy* at all. Consequences justify blame directly without positing the useless intermediary of blameworthiness. A 'reductionist' strategy would hold that those blamed are blameworthy but that being blameworthy *just is* being a person whom it would be morally permissible to blame. Either way, blameworthiness need not be ascribed to the persons we blame in any murky, metaphysical way that stands opposed to Strawsonian subjectivism.

We could offer a similar view, with the same distinction between elimination and reduction, from the perspective of contractarian theory. On this view, we justifiably may blame persons simply because they violate implicit moral contracts to desist from certain behaviors, without positing the metaphysical quality of blameworthiness. As the consequentialist could also say, what we care about is justifying blame, and we do that when we complete the formula: "Those persons we blame are blamed justifiably if and only if _____." If we can do this by citing the tenets of a moral theory, then we have accomplished what we have set out to do. It is obtuse to insist that the blank must be filled in by citing a metaphysical property of those we blame, because the only point of talking about blameworthiness is to enable us to complete the formula. If we can complete it without citing metaphysical blameworthiness, so much the worse for metaphysics.

Strawson's critic will reply that so long as we try to justify blame on *any* grounds that are external to agents—such as favorable consequences or implicit contracts—rather than because persons are intrinsically blameworthy, blame is unjust. Strawson expresses his dissatisfaction with consequentialist rationales for blame (1962, 61–62), but the same degree of dissatisfaction logically should arise if we try to justify blame by reference to contractarian rationales *or* by claiming that reactive attitudes are a deep fact about human psychology. If it is not enough to be told that the blame we receive is justified because it contributes to the greater good of our society (thereby raising the scapegoating objection to consequentialism), then it is not enough to be told that blame reveals a deep tendency of blamers (or even those blamed themselves) to feel and express their reactive attitudes. In both cases, whether we talk about justification or not, we try to account for blame by citing facts that are extrinsic to the person blamed. This intuition will be most strongly felt if we consider the plea of someone who denies having acted freely: "True, I have violated contracts, it has beneficial consequences to blame and punish me, and doing so expresses an important aspect of the human psyche. But unless *I* am blameworthy, I do not deserve this treatment, and it is unfair to blame and punish me."

The debate so far has proved to be a specific instance of the debate over whether moral objectivity (in this case, moral responsibility) can be secured without presupposing extra-psychological, metaphysical entities (God's will, Platonic moral truths, non-natural moral properties, etc.) to establish that objectivity. Non-nihilistic subjectivists believe that widely shared feelings about morality constitute a sufficient basis to justify morality. Nihilistic subjectivists think that the claim that morality is nothing beyond (more or less widely shared) moral intuitions shows that in moral matters no opinion can be better than all the others.

Bringing this general dispute to bear on the specific question of blame, let us ask why the premise that blame requires justification by the intrinsic quality of blameworthiness inspires visceral assent from Strawson's critics and a yawn from Strawson's supporters. How can this claim appear to be an important truth to the former and utterly misguided to the latter? The answer may lie in metaphilosophical differences.

Although I confess I am not entirely sure, I assume that Strawson does not intend to completely reject the idea of justifying moral responsibility ascriptions. (Strawson's rejection of consequentialist justifications of blame suggests that he takes justification seriously.) If so, then the trick is to see how Strawson's subjectivism can provide *any* justificatory force. I believe that this can happen if and only if Strawson relies on Philosophy as Providing Underpinnings or Philosophy as Praxis or a combination of these views. From a descriptive standpoint, persons and their commonsense characteristics, including freedom and responsibility, are the subject matter about which we philosophize. To use philosophy to overturn its base would lie somewhere between irony and absurdity. From a normative standpoint, the importance and, hence, the existence of value is not to be undone by analyses of value. This, too, would make no clear sense. Finding out through philosophical investigation that blame is subjective to blamers *couldn't* have the deflationary consequences that Strawson's critic supposes, because neither Philosophy as Praxis nor Philosophy as Underpinning Common Sense permits a conclusion that undermines philosophy's reason for being.

If we instead appeal to the view of Philosophy as Worldview Construction, then Strawson's subjectivism seems to lead to nihilism. Worldview Construction, which questions all commonsense beliefs, demands to know how freedom and responsibility can be 'fit' onto those parts of the world that are not persons' attitudes and feelings. This demand drives the libertarians to propose indeterminacy in order to explain how persons could be truly responsible for their acts, and it drives the hard determinists and subjectivists such as me to deny moral responsibility. Such views—which seem metaphysically extreme to the advocates of Philosophy as Underpinnings and Philosophy as Praxis—to their own advocates appear not even to demand *deep* responsibility, but merely *real* responsibility. To Worldview thinkers, to learn that blameworthiness has no existence external to the attitudes of blamers would be to be disabused of one's belief in blameworthiness, no less than learning a similar truth about the Loch Ness monster would undercut our belief in it. According to World-view Construction, because subjectivism denies the objectivity of moral responsibility, and because moral responsibility must be objective in order for there to be a distinction between apparent and real responsibility, subjectivism implies that moral responsibility is not real.

5. The Debate over Dual Rationality

Libertarians believe that at least some free choices are undetermined, whether these thinkers seek to guarantee that we have a categorical abil-ity to choose otherwise than we do or that we are the ultimate causes of our choices. This two-way ability must be shown to be desirable whether the libertarian account is presented in terms of event causation (Kane, 1985 and 1996) or agent causation (Clarke, 1993; O'Connor, 1995A). This means that both choices that the libertarian theory posits as physi-cally possible must meet satisfactory standards for being under the rational control of the chooser. In this century, compatibilists such as R. Hobart, M. Schlick, and A. J. Ayer have complained that an undetermined choice must be capricious, whimsical, irrational—indeed, not even a *choice* of a libertarian agent but an unpredictable, random event that happens *in* the agent. Kane poses the problem less hyperbolically: How can we under-stand how exactly *one* deliberative process can produce *two* diametri-cally opposed choices that are both reasonable (1985, 57)?

It is important to appreciate how the issue of the rationality of liber-tarian choices enters into the free will discussion. The central question is this: "*Would a libertarian agent enjoy dual rationality in a robust enough way to be morally responsible for choice A and choice not-A, whichever occurs?*" For instance, if a man makes a libertarian-style choice where it is 0.4 likely that he will commit a murder and 0.6 likely that he will refrain, is the man sufficiently in rational control of *both* outcomes to be free and morally responsible for whichever results? It is easy to allow the discus-sion of the rationality of libertarian choices to drift away from this central issue onto tangents about rationality and explanation in general. My only interest in discussing the rationality of libertarian choices, however, lies in addressing the specific question given above.

Kane sought to address the challenge by specifying the conditions under which an undetermined choice could be dual rational—that is, would be rational whichever of the two ways it went. In *Free Will and Values*, Kane held that persons can enjoy ultimate dominion over their indeterminate choices provided that "the agent's making the choice rather than doing otherwise (or vice versa . . .) can be explained by saying that the agent rationally willed at t to do so" (1985, 46). Kane also gave an explicit recipe for dual rationality, which he updated in his reply to my 1988 paper:

> The choice of A by an agent is *dual rational*, if and only if, *whichever way it goes* . . . the outcome is (a) the intentional termination of an effort of will that is the agent's . . . (b) the agent has reasons for the choice (which-ever occurs), (c) the agent does it *for* those reasons, and (d) given the agent's character and motives, it is, all things considered, rational for the agent to do it at that time for those reasons. (1988, 446)

Consider Kane's example of a difficult moral choice (1988, 449–54). Suppose that an agent's choice of altruistic alternative A or self-serving alternative S depends on the degree of effort she makes to adopt the moral point of view, and that the degree of effort she manages is metaphysically undetermined. Her termination of the effort, by opting for the altruistic option or by giving in to the self-serving one, *is* her choice. There is no deterministic explanation of her choice, because the termination of her struggle coincides with the chaotically amplified result of an undetermined quantum event in her brain. Thus, the termination of the struggle is psychophysically *identical* to the process begun by the amplified quantum event. If the quantum event occurs at one second, she manages the effort to opt for altruism; if it does not, she goes the other way.

According to Kane, as evinced in his principle of dual rationality given above, citing her (good) reasons for and against each alternative and the struggle that she undergoes suffices to explain rationally whichever alternative is chosen. As Kane emphasizes, these are *her* reasons, *her* struggle and *her* effort. Because she has gone through a moral struggle with her conflicting motivations, no one is likely to call her whimsical, irrational, or capricious, however the decision goes. Most important, her choice of either the altruistic or self-serving reasons make those her most weighty reasons *at the time she makes the choice*, although not before the choice is made. Hence, in Kanian free willings there is no liberty of indifference. It is not as if one state of affairs could produce two diametrically opposed outcomes, as in Kane's example where all my careful deliberations point to choosing to vacation in Hawaii and I inexplicably choose to go to Colorado instead. Whether I choose A or S, I choose for the reasons that are the most powerful for me at the time I choose.

I have a direct response to this very attractive example. By my lights of what constitutes an adequate explanation—for my purposes in this context—until we assign probabilities, we can provide *no* adequate explanation of A or S. By hypothesis, which alternative occurs depends on a quantum event whose occurrence was not caused to occur when it did. Given Kane's description of the example, it is fair to say that the termination of the agent's moral struggle at whatever time the quantum event occurs was *intentional*, because the agent was deliberating. Nonetheless, nothing among the agent's psychological states causes the quantum event to happen at exactly one time rather than another. Therefore, although we may come to understand a great deal about the agent's deliberations by learning psychological facts about her, we will never reach the point where we see why either choice results rather than the one that does not, because *the agent's psychological condition before she made the choice* did not establish whether A or S occurred. *Quantum indeterminacy* did.

I think that the case should be described this way: "The agent experienced conflicting motivations. She struggled to pick the altruistic alternative against her strong inclination to select the self-serving one. She tried her best, but why she managed the degree of effort that produced the actual choice and not the other is a mystery, inasmuch as it was traceable to an undetermined quantum event, for which there is no telling why it occurred when it did. Our lack of understanding why the quantum event happened just when it did disables our ability to understand why the exact outcome that depended on it was that way."

In Kane's example, the amount of moral effort that the agent musters is not determined by her character and motives (1988, 449). Kane thinks, though, that both possible indeterminate degrees of effort that may result will be *explained* by citing the agent's psychological states. To support this he writes: "[T]he complex of past motives and character explains the inner *conflict* from *both* sides. It explains why the agent makes the effort *and* also why it is an effort" (1988, 450). But these are very different issues: (1) why the agent makes the effort, (2) why it is an effort, and (3) why the actual effort was made. Issues (1) and (2) can be explained by reference to the agent's motives and character. By hypothesis, however, the degree of effort expended is not caused by those motives and character. In such a case we may be able to say enough about the agent's choice to produce a sense of familiarity with it. But given the supposition of indeterminism, *relative to the agent's motives and character*, the degree of effort managed (and hence the choice) turns out to be a matter of chance.

To avoid this objection, the libertarian does not need to say that we have an informative explanation of the choice only if the degree of effort is *determined* by the motives and character, but there needs to be a bottom limit on the connection between motives and character on one side and the effort on the other. This suggests that the connection should be greater than 0.5. (See my Principle of Rational Explanation in Double, 1988B; 1991B; 1993.) But if we accept this demand, given the premise that the probabilities of A and not-A cannot both be greater than 0.5, we must conclude that libertarian choices cannot be rational in both directions.

Throughout this discussion I have assumed that the possibility of two-way rational choices entails the logical possibility of there being *contrastive explanations* for each outcome. I demand that there can be true explanations (whether anyone can produce them is irrelevant) of libertarian choices that cite facts about the world and would explain both why A happens rather than not-A (if A happens) and why not-A happens rather than A (if not-A happens). I realize that what I have demanded of the libertarian logically cannot be met. As David Lewis notes, when we are talking about probabilistic explanation we cannot even explain *one* outcome contrastively, let alone more than one:

> The actual causal history of the actual chance outcome does not differ at all from the unactualized causal history that the other outcome would have had, if that outcome had happened. A contrastive why-question with "rather" requests information about the feature that differentiate the actual causal history from its counterfactual alternative. There are no such features, so the question can have no positive answer. Thus we are right to call chance events inexplicable, if it is contrastive explanation that we have in mind. (1993, 197)

Having this much settled, the question becomes whether my demand for contrastive explanations of libertarian choices is reasonable. Kane and Randolph Clarke think that it certainly is not. Kane suggests that because no libertarian theory can provide contrastive explanations of choices, my demand is question-begging (1996, chapter 10). Clarke (1992) punctuates his rejection of my demand for contrastive explanations by imagining a case where he has compelling reasons for choosing to go to the beach and for choosing to go to the mountains. Although "there will be no contrastive explanation . . . that would answer the question . . . "Why did you go to the beach rather than to the mountains?" . . . [s]uch actions are nevertheless rationally explicable. . . . There is nothing rationally defective about an action of this sort" (1993, 196).

Other libertarians have thought that both outcomes of indeterminist choices can be given sensible explanations when we experience "the liberty of indifference." In "The Dilemma of Determinism" William James (1962, 155–57) gives as an example his indifferent choosing to walk home after his lecture by Divinity Avenue or Oxford Street. James asks us to imagine that indeterminism is true and, hence, that if the cosmos could be rerun back to the time of the choice, both options could be selected. In this counterfactual situation, James writes, "either universe *after the fact* and once there would, to our means of observation and understanding, appear just as rational as the other" (1962, 156). That is, we could tell a convincing narrative on behalf of whatever outcome resulted. The determinist critic of the rationality of indeterminate choices would have to say that one of these choices was irrational; but James thinks that common sense is clearly on his side in this dispute.

Compare next Clarke's and James's views on explanations to Thomas Nagel's argument that having a decent idea of why we chose one option requires that we be able to explain why we chose that option instead of not choosing it. According to Nagel, for the libertarian

> [a] free action . . . should be fully explained only intentionally, in terms of justifying reasons and purposes. When someone makes an autonomous choice such as whether to accept a job, and there are reasons on both sides of the issue, we are supposed to be able to explain what he did by pointing to his reasons for accepting it. But we could equally have explained his refusing the job, if he had refused, by referring to the reasons on the other side—and he could have refused it for those reasons: that is the essential claim of autonomy. It applies even if one choice is significantly more reasonable than the other. Bad reasons are reasons too.
>
> Intentional explanation . . . can explain either choice in terms of the appropriate reasons, since either choice would be intelligible if it occurred. But for this very reason it cannot explain why the person accepted the job for the reasons in favor instead of refusing it for the reasons against it. It cannot explain on grounds of intelligibility why one of two intelligible courses of action, both of which are possible, occurred. (1986, 115–16)

I realize that philosophers of science are divided on the question of what qualities a good explanation needs (Lipton, 1991, chapter 2), and I accept Clarke's claim that defenders of the contrastiveness requirement are in the minority (Clarke, 1992, 3–6). I am not worried by these admissions, however, because when I am discussing the dual rationality of libertarian choices I am concerned not with explanation but with the quality of the connection between libertarian agents and their two-way, uncaused choices. If our interest is in moral responsibility, the key question is whether in cases of libertarian indeterminism we can be enough in control of undetermined choices to be morally responsible for *both* outcomes. To illustrate my claim I propose a thought experiment.

In this example you are torn between conflicting reasons for choosing to avenge what you believe was your uncle's murder of your father and for choosing to refrain from murder. As the moment when you have to decide approaches, your reasons for refraining begin to get the upper hand. Just then, unbeknownst to you, a very powerful demon who has been monitoring your deliberative struggle deactivates the part of your neural firing that constitutes your pro-refraining cognitions. As a result, your pro-murder reasons are left standing by default as the only effective reasons, and you murder your uncle.

According to everything that you can know introspectively, you have ample evidence for thinking that you know why you chose as you did. Citing your pro-murder reasons would be a paradigm of a reasons-explanation. But because of the unusual causal circumstances, your ignorance makes your reasons-explanation defective. Unless we cite the role of the demon in deactivating your stronger reasons in favor of abstaining, we do not know why you chose to murder your uncle, and we do not really know why your uncle is dead. We may know your reasons, and knowing that you were capable of such reasons might justify our having an unfavorable moral opinion of you. But in fairness to you, your pro-murder reasons, though deplorable, were not the last word about you. *Your* reasons were not *the* reason for your choice in the sense of being everything we need to know to understand why it happened. Without the demon's intervention you would have chosen not to murder, and if anyone is morally responsible for the murder, it is the demon, not you. Thus, the demon's role must be included in any account that tells whether you deserve moral censure. Regardless of how understandable the choice you made seems to you or to third persons generally, it is not enough to cite reasons that were less than 0.5 likely to produce the actual choice made and managed to produce the choice only due to factors that did not depend on your psychological states.

I claim that if we are concerned with moral responsibility regarding choices, the above theme holds for improbable reason-sets generally, whether a demon enables them to be effective or whether they come out on top due to indeterminism. For any choice whose probability is less than 0.5, there has to be a contrastive explanation of why that improbable alternative was realized. It is not enough to cite the fact that the agent has reasons for it, just as it is not enough to cite your pro-murder reasons without including the role of the demon in blocking your reasons for abstaining.

Let me summarize what I think is going on in this debate. Relative to my demand for contrastive explanations of libertarian two-way choices in order to ensure that agents are in control of both alternatives, libertarian choices necessarily fail. Indeterminists may resist that demand in several ways. One way is to weaken the requirements for adequate explanations to what is called *teleological intelligibility*. As Nagel notes, on this notion, explanations of human behavior become easy, but at the expense of contrastiveness. A second way is to endorse probabilistic explanation as a reputable species of scientific explanation that explicitly rejects the need for contrastive explanations, as Clarke does. These two forms of explanation may converge (if we think that reasons are probabilistic causes) or diverge (if we think that reasons-explanations exclude causal explanations of even a probabilistic sort.) Either way, teleological intelligibility and probabilistic notions of explanation share the common theme that contrastive explanations are not required of libertarian choices. To thinkers who endorse either view I ask why the fact that non-contrastive explanations are used in *other* areas of our intellectual lives counts against my claim that contrastive explanations are needed when we try to justify holding persons morally responsible for uncaused decisions (e.g., to murder and not to murder).

So far, the main issue boils down to this: Does the dual rationality needed to allow libertarian agents to be free and morally responsible in two directions require that each choice be capable of being explained contrastively? Although, as I have urged, this is not a question about explanation (but rather one that depends on a moral intuition), it is inevitable that our answer to it will be influenced by our ideas about explanation, and these ideas may even impede our recognition that it *is* a moral question. This leads to our meta-level views. My demand that human choices have contrastive explanations before they can be deeply reflective of who we are is influenced by my attraction to Hempelian ideas about explanation. Although I agree that the notion of *explaining choice c* is not semantically equivalent to *explaining why choice not-c is not chosen*, I think that to have a deep understanding of why c comes about that will support the ascription of free will, we must be able to say why not-c is not chosen. But this is not the only approach we may take.

Suppose we think that social science is the business of telling plausible-sounding folk-psychological narratives that create a feeling of comfortableness with previously surprising data. (Recall Camus's 1955 claim that even atomic theory is poetry.) Suppose we extend that attitude to philosophy in general, arrive at Philosophy as Conversation, and say that philosophical explanations are, at their best, the telling of interesting, plausible-sounding stories. In this case, my demand for contrastive explanations even in this special case involving moral responsibility will seem too strong, because *all* philosophical explanations will be seen as teleological intelligibility explanations.

If we are libertarians with Praxis motivations, we may not be able to get past the moral repercussions of the demand for contrastiveness in order for us to be responsible for libertarian choices. Philosophers who endorse Philosophy as Underpinning Common Sense or Philosophy as Underpinning Science would be predisposed in favor of the criteria of adequacy of explanations that seems preferred by common sense or science. On the latter metaphilosophy, the fact that non-contrastive explanations are scientifically reputable might cause an Underpinnings theorist to become impatient with a demand for contrastiveness in the discussion of the possibility of libertarian dual control.

5

How the Free Will
Debate Depends
on Metaphilosophy (II)

In this chapter I continue to illustrate the way that recent discussions of the free will problem depend on disagreements over metaphilosophy and intermediate-level philosophical principles. In section 1, I display an analogy between normative ethics and meta-ethics on the one side and lower-level free will theorizing and the metaphysics of free will on the other. Metaphilosophical moves available to the normative theorist who lacks a meta-ethical solution are mirrored by those available to free will theorists who lack a solution to the problem of the metaphysics of free will. In section 2, I argue that the importance of Peter van Inwagen's celebrated consequence argument depends squarely on metaphilosophical premises. In section 3, I make the same case in a different way regarding Harry Frankfurt's equally famous principle of alternative possibilities. In section 4, I examine the question of whether philosophers should endorse a sliding scale of demands for various philosophical subject matters or whether they should demand equal proof for all philosophical claims. In that section I consider some arguments from Thomas Nagel and J. R. Lucas. In section 5, I argue that Peter French's non-standard view of the relation between moral responsibility and ascriptions of moral responsibility is plausible just in case we adopt a non-standard meta-philosophy.

1. The Analogy between the Metaphysics
of Ethics and the Metaphysics of Free Will

Some philosophers who see no answer to the question of how there could be moral truth propound normative theories anyway. Hume provided perhaps the definitive case for moral non-realism, concluding that morals have no firmer foundation than sentiments, but subscribed to a utilitarian theory of normative ethics. Mill, admitting that there can be no proof that anything is desirable beyond the fact that it is desired, provided one of the classic elaborations of a normative system. We might view the combining of non-realist metaethics and normative ethical theory with approval or disapproval.

From the negative side, we could emphasize the intellectual schizophrenia involved in the moral non-realist's acceptance of normative theory. According to this criticism, unless we have what we take to be an adequate rebuttal to moral non-realism, we should (logically) feel sheepish about espousing normative theories, for moral non-realism appears to undo our normative theory. A person who propounds normative theory while accepting moral non-realism certainly can do so in a way that invites the charge of schizophrenia. For instance, this charge would look apt if we said, "I just don't care about the conflict. I know what I believe, and I leave the task of reconciling my beliefs to someone else." But there are several avenues open to the non-realist/normative theorist besides this know-nothing reply.

First, there is no inconsistency, logical or otherwise, in saying that morality has its only basis in human feelings and then trying to give a theoretical system of ethics that is predicated on and systematizes those feelings. This would be no more odd than admitting that what persons find to be humorous depends on the subjective psychological states of audiences and then going on to give a theoretical account of what makes persons laugh. Second, we cannot object to presenting a normative theory in a fallibilistic spirit: "In case I am wrong about moral non-realism, here is the theory of normative ethics that I believe has the best chance of being true." Third, it makes sense for a moral non-realist to give a normative theory on the grounds that we are psychologically bound to *act* as if ethics has a deeper foundation than human sentiment, even if we intellectually conclude that it cannot. On this supposition, our belief in the objectivity of morality at those times when we face moral problems would be seen as "cognitively impenetrable" to our meta-ethical conclusions.

The sort of dynamic just described holds also in the case of the metaphysics of free will and specific free will theories such as compatibilism or incompatibilism. In meta-ethics we ask whether there can be moral truth, and in normative ethics we ask what that truth is. In the metaphysics of free will we ask whether our judgments about the freeness of choices can be objectively true. On the metaphysical realist position I hold, the possibility of those judgments being true depends on whether there could be a mind-independent characteristic of 'freeness' that free choices have and unfree choices lack. So the possibility that *free choice* denotes depends on whether there could exist an objective characteristic of being free. In arguing for such positions as libertarianism, hard determinism, or soft determinism, we presuppose a positive answer to this metaphysical question and try to construct the best answer we can as to what free choices *would* be like, on the supposition that free choices *could* exist. Thus, as with normative ethics, our lower-level answer is jeopardized by a negative answer to the meta-level question.

The distinction between the metaphysics of free will and substantive free will theories is not as widely recognized as the distinction between meta-ethics and normative ethics, but I believe that this is due to historical happenstance. If philosophers were to read the free will literature with this distinction in mind, the distinction would appear before their eyes. This is true despite the fact that many free will theorists address both questions, just as many moral theorists discuss both meta-ethics and normative ethics without explicitly distinguishing between them. It is also true despite the fact that more effort has been spent on specific free will theories than on the metaphysics of free will. (Robert Kane [1996] explicitly discusses the metaphysics of free will under his rubric of the *intelligibility* of free will.)

Just as we could approve or disapprove of trying to provide moral theories in absence of an answer to the meta-ethical problem, we could approve or disapprove of trying to provide lower-level free will theories in absence of a general answer to the question of how free will is possible. On the negative side, again, we could make the charge of intellectual schizophrenia. Until we can explain how there could be moral responsibility (a paradigm of a moral property) or how the 'characteristic' of being free could be anything more than the favorable ratings we give to certain choices, as good epistemic agents we should suspend judgment on theories such as compatibilism or incompatibilism. We lack philosophical candor if we treat free will as if it is real when our best intellectual investigation suggests that it is not.

In this case, as with ethics, we could respond in a know-nothing fashion. But here too we can provide better replies. The three justifications given in the ethics example can be modified to produce reasons for propounding substantive free will theories in absence of an answer to the problem regarding the metaphysics of free will.

First, we could interpret specific free will theories as explicating our feelings about free will without supposing that there is any objective sense to be made out of *free will*. The free will problem thereby would be viewed as the explication of both the 'phenomenology' and the concepts of freedom, rather than an attempt to construct a worldview. Much of Galen Strawson's *Freedom and Belief* (1986) examines free will from this perspective. Strawson himself thinks that both compatibilists and incompatibilists are bound to fail to show how we can be deeply responsible for our choices. But a philosopher *could* analyze the concepts and phenomenology of free will without worrying at all about the debate between the compatibilists and incompatibilists. Someone, for example, who sees this sort of investigation as interesting conversation or as helpful in underpinning common sense.

The second, fallibilistic, tack can be expressed by various metaphilosophers, including those who are moved by seeing philosophy as Worldview Construction: "I am not sure whether the idea of free choice makes sense or not, but here is my best proposal in case it does." High-minded and honest, this approach allows inquiry to proceed, without endorsing free will. I am unable to think of an actual philosopher who falls into this category, although it seems to me a very sensible view.

The third justification holds that we are bound to think and act as if persons are sometimes free and sometimes not. Therefore, we need to produce an account that fits those beliefs and actions, even if we cannot give a theoretically satisfying account. Especially relevant is the claim that we are going to continue to hold persons morally responsible and feel reactive attitudes toward them as long as we view persons as persons. Perhaps the strongest way to support this third line is by combining two metaphilosophical themes. Philosophy as Praxis would suggest that skeptical worries ought to be rejected, on the premise that producing free will theories is a morally valuable contribution for philosophers to make. Philosophy as Underpinnings is relevant also because common sense endorses the reality of free choice and moral responsibility. Praxis and Philosophy as Underpinning Common Sense can be combined to downplay the importance of the intellectual schizophrenia that the critics find objectionable. Daniel Dennett combines Praxis and Underpinnings of Common Sense motivations when he offers a facile analogy in response to the incompatibilist worry about holding morally responsible persons who may be determined:

> Our refusal, beyond some arbitrary point, to delve further into causes and circumstances may strike a chord of suspicion in some. Can this policy be fair? Indeed it can. Remember that the breaks average out; we could not improve basketball by disallowing the fluke shots and unlucky breaks. (My claim here is in effect that *holding people responsible is the best game in town*.) (1984, 162)

If we run together the 'would' and 'should' questions as Peter Strawson does in the following passage, we see another combination of Praxis and Underpinnings motivations:

> [R]eactive attitudes are essentially natural human reactions to the good or ill will or indifference of others towards us, as displayed in *their* attitudes and actions. The question we have to ask is: What effect would, or should, the acceptance of . . . determinism have upon these reactive attitudes? More specifically, would, or should, the acceptance of the truth of the thesis lead to the decay or the repudiation of all such attitudes? . . .
> I am strongly inclined to think that it is, for us as we are, practically inconceivable. The human commitment to participation in ordinary inter-personal relationships is, I think, too thoroughly and deeply rooted for us to take seriously the thought that a general theoretical conviction might so change our world. (1962, 67–68)

There is a fourth way that someone might use metaphilosophy to justify espousing free will theories without having to address the metaphysical problem. Philosophy as Conversation sees no need to take seriously the meta-level worries, whether in the metaphysics of ethics or in the metaphysics of free will. According to Conversation metaphilosophy, philosophy should get out of the business of trying to produce foundations (for morality or anything else), because it lacks the credibility to pull off such portentous (and pretentious) super-critiques. Rather than acknowledging that the metaphysics of free will produces a difficulty for our selection of a free will theory, the Conversation theorist may elect to dismiss the meta-level question as pedantic and boring. Just as Conversation theorists reject the fact-value distinction, believing that meta-ethics is a degenerate form of conversation, they may feel likewise about the meta-level worries over free will.

2. Van Inwagen's Consequence Argument

We can characterize the free will problem in terms that are analogous to Thomas Kuhn's (1962) distinction between normal science and revolutionary science. Normal science is done by scientists who share a dominant paradigm or model of both what exists and how good scientists investigate it, while revolutionary science is done by those scientists whose practice violates an accepted paradigm. The traditional disputants in the free will debate—the libertarians, hard determinists, soft determinists, incompatibilists, and compatibilists—are practitioners of 'normal philosophy.' These thinkers share the belief that *free will* and *moral responsibility* can denote and agree that the free will problem consists in figuring out the conditions under which these terms *would* denote. Opposed to these theorists are practitioners of 'revolutionary philosophy' who claim, as I do, that these terms are defective.

The free will debate is full of powerful examples of normal philosophy by philosophers who assume that *free will* and *moral responsibility* can have objective reference. The visceral intuition that we cannot be 'truly' deserving of blame for our actions if we are not their ultimate cause is plied skillfully by both defenders and opponents of moral responsibility such as Peter van Inwagen (1983), Robert Kane (1985), Galen Strawson (1986), and Bruce Waller (1990). On the other side, the compatibilist reply that ultimate self-causation is not desirable but represents, in Dennett's terms, "a purely metaphysical hankering" is made forcefully by Dennett (1984, 163), Harry Frankfurt (1969; 1971), and Gary Watson (1975).

Van Inwagen's widely discussed consequence argument shows how incompatibilists can use the tools of analytic philosophy such as modal logic and possible-worlds semantics to support their view. Anyone who enters into the voluminous debate begun by some papers by van Inwagen (van Inwagen, 1974; 1975; 1980) and then his *Essay on Free Will* (van Inwagen, 1983) can easily forget the inductive lesson that substantive philosophical problems seldom yield to anyone's clever use of technical machinery.

In his book, van Inwagen begins his incompatibilist argument with a vivid summary: "If determinism is true, then our acts are the consequences of the laws of nature and events in the remote past. But it is not up to us what went on before we were born, and neither is it up to us what the laws of nature are. Therefore, the consequences of these things (including our present acts) are not up to us" (1983, 56).

After fifty pages of careful analysis of three versions of this argument, van Inwagen concludes: "If determinism is true, no one can act otherwise than he does. If determinism is true, no one has it within his power to realize any possibility that is in fact unrealized. If determinism is true, no one has any choice about anything. In short, if determinism is true, there is no free will" (1983, 106).

I want to go directly to the version of the consequence argument that deals with moral responsibility without considering the rest of the argument. For one thing, the argument has been scrutinized in detail by first-rate analytic philosophers such as David Lewis (1981), Michael Slote (1982), Terence Horgan (1985), and John Martin Fischer (1986B), and I have nothing to add to their examinations. For another, I believe that the most important part of the argument comes *after* van Inwagen concludes that if determinism is true, then no one can act otherwise.

On the one hand, there is a sense in which the consequence argument is obviously sound, inasmuch as the conclusion that no one can act otherwise—in one important sense—is a deductive consequence of van Inwagen's definition of *determinism*. Van Inwagen defines *determinism* as the thesis that due to the laws of nature, there is only one physically possible future (1983, 65). It follows, then, that *if* determinism is the case, all events, including all human choices, are the logical consequences of the laws of nature and prior conditions. We have to agree, then, that *if* being able to choose otherwise requires physically open alternatives, determinism implies that no one can choose otherwise. I see nothing problematic about drawing this conclusion from the concept *determinism*.

It is also clear that our inability to choose otherwise in the sense that we lack physically open alternatives gives no support to the view that we would have not have chosen otherwise *had some condition been different than it was*—for example, if we had wanted to choose otherwise. Determinism implies that had some other relevant condition obtained, the determining sequence would have been different and a different choice would have been made. As van Inwagen notes (1989, 404), "[W]ho could deny that at most moments each of us is such that he would then be acting differently if he had chosen to act differently?" Determinism does not entail that our choices would be the same if we had not wanted to make them.

Therefore, there is a sense in which determinism entails that we could not have chosen otherwise and a sense in which it does not. Determinism disallows a 'kind' of freedom (libertarian free will) and allows another kind (compatibilist free will.) The important question, which logically cannot be addressed by debating whether the premises of the consequence argument show that determinism implies that we cannot act differently, is this: Which *kind* of freedom is necessary for moral responsibility? How threatened should we *feel* by the fact that determinism would eliminate libertarian choices? Or how *pleased* should we be, given the problems that have been alleged against libertarian choices?

Daniel Dennett argues from the (true) premise that we cannot know whether persons experience libertarian or compatibilist free will to the conclusion that to ask which is better is pointless (1984, 136–37). Seeing things from the perspective of Philosophy as Worldview Construction, I do not think that the unanswerability of a question makes it pointless. The problem, as I see it, is that the question of whether libertarian or compatibilist free will is more desirable calls on us to make an evaluation, which we subjectivists believe can rely on nothing more than our attitudes toward determined choices. No use of modal logic is of any help here.

Let me support my claim. In his three versions of the consequence argument in chapter 2 of *An Essay on Free Will*, van Inwagen casts the argument in terms of whether we could have done otherwise and in terms of whether we have the power to actualize unactualized possible worlds if determinism is true. I believe that when the consequence argument is cast in these terms, the attitudinal disagreement described above will prevent us from reaching a final conclusion in favor of the compatibilist or the incompatibilist. But in chapter 5 van Inwagen writes explicitly about moral responsibility as he did in his 1980 article by claiming that no one is morally responsible if determinism is true. Crucial to the argument is inference rule (B), which claims that non-responsibility 'transfers' from the past to our present actions if determinism is true: From $N(p>q)$ and Np we may infer Nq. I understand this to mean: If p implies q and no one is, or ever has been, even partly responsible for the fact that p implies q, and p obtains and no one is, or ever has been, even partly responsible for the fact that p obtains, then it logically follows that no one is, or ever was, responsible for q (1983, 184; 1980, 32). Van Inwagen believes that (B) can sanction the chain of inferences from the fact that we are not responsible for the laws of nature and conditions in the distant past to the conclusion that we are not responsible for the present causal products of those factors (i.e., our choices and actions).

Van Inwagen admits that (B) is not provable. He also notes that its citing a moral notion counts against its provability, because inference forms using moral notions are unlikely to be reducible to generally accepted non-moral inference forms (1980, 34). Nonetheless, van Inwagen claims that (B) is much more plausible than its denial. But how can we be confident about such a moral claim? It is easy to imagine how (B) might be false. Suppose we said that (B) is acceptable, *except* in those cases where an agent's self-reflective choice is causally effective in the transition from p to q? On this view, determined persons may be located between remote causes and present determined effects yet be morally responsible for the latter, provided their contribution to the choice meets some rationality-based compatibilist account of freedom (Blumenfeld, 1988; Double, 1991B, chapter 2). It all depends on whether the internal quality of the choice is *good enough* to make us responsible.

Because I am not a compatibilist, I do not really believe that this tack shows (B) to be false. As a moral subjectivist I think that (B) lacks a truth-value altogether. Nonetheless, considering this reply shows that the steps that got us to the conclusion of the consequence argument do not settle what we want to settle regarding moral responsibility, the prize of the free will problem. We are forced back to a conflict of intuitions. We may not notice this if we remain focused on the narrow debate within normal philosophy, but once we step back, the point is striking.

If the technical apparatus used in the consequence argument cannot help us interpret its conclusion, then what can? For van Inwagen the answer appears to lie in his appeal to intuitions. It just seems to van Inwagen that inference rule (B) is right, and he cannot think of any clear counter-example to (B) (van Inwagen, 1980, 34). (The compatibilist's intuition that satisfactory ratiocination enables us to be responsible seems not to count.) How can we justify relying on our intuitions and rejecting those of others? Notoriously, relying on intuitions in normative ethics is risky. Recall J. J. C. Smart's suggestion (1973, 68–69) that when our moral intuitions run contrary to the tenets of our ethical theory, we can just as well give up the intuitions as give up the theory. Can the appeal to intuitions in this case have any greater justification?

The reliance on intuitions gains credibility from meta-level factors, possibly from a combination of sources. There is the non-skeptical intermediate-level principle that endorses intuitions as a way of securing foundations for our theoretical endeavors; this principle may be endorsed by any of the four metaphilosophies. From Philosophy as Underpinning Common Sense we may derive the dictum: It is only commonsensical to treat our intuitions as evidence, even with respect to rarified philosophical debates such as that over (B). From Philosophy as Praxis we may think that because we morally *have* to decide whether determinism destroys free will, when intuitions are our last source of evidence, we should go with our intuitions rather than remaining in an indecisive intellectual quandary.

3. Frankfurt's Principle of Alternative Possibilities

There is another way in which the free will problem may be viewed in terms of *normal* vs. *revolutionary philosophy*. Compatibilism prospers when we frame the free will problem so that it can be settled by carefully examining our everyday ideas about freedom. In our prephilosophical thought about freedom we assume that persons choose freely unless some unusual factor intrudes. The assumption that free will has default status runs through Aristotle, Hobbes, Locke, Hume, Mill, and most twentieth-century compatibilists. Perhaps the most influential recent development of this theme is Harry Frankfurt's (1969) celebrated argument that metaphysically open alternative possibilities are not necessary for us to be morally responsible for our actions.

In Frankfurt's best-known example, Black, a powerful manipulator, is able to cause Jones to act as Black wishes *if* Jones begins to choose differently than Black wishes. Therefore, in the case where Jones chooses as Black wishes (and Black does not intervene), Black's potential for controlling Jones's choice guarantees that Jones could not have done otherwise than he did. But surely, Frankfurt believes, the mere fact that Jones could not have done otherwise because of Black's potential agency casts no doubt on Jones's moral responsibility in those cases where Black does not intervene. Generalizing from this example, Frankfurt concludes that moral responsibility does not require incompatibilism's physically open alternatives. "The principle of alternative possibilities should thus be replaced," according to Frankfurt, with the view that "a person is not morally responsible for what he has done if he did it *only because* he could not have done otherwise" (1969, 838, my italics). According to Frankfurt, agents in a determined universe without metaphysically open alternative possibilities may select actions because they *want* to perform them, not only because they are determined to perform them. Thus, for Frankfurt, incompatibilists cannot use the (correctly) revised principle of alternative possibilities to argue that determinism per se creates any difficulty for moral responsibility.

An interesting dialectic occurs when Frankfurt-examples are pitted against van Inwagen's consequence argument. Mark Ravizza (1994) argues that Frankfurt-type examples can be used to discredit van Inwagen's apparently plausible transfer of non-responsibility principle (B) discussed in the last section. Ravizza asks us to consider these cases: (1) A non-personal agent such as a goat knocking over a stone simultaneously over-determines an individual's intentional causing an avalanche by using explosives. (2) A second agent simultaneously over-determines the action of a first agent, as in the case where a second assassin also fatally wounds a victim.

Ravizza claims that the agents whose actions were over-determined by other factors in cases (1) and (2) were at least partially morally responsible for their actions, despite the fact that they were not at all responsible for the alternative sequences of events that led to the avalanche or assassination. Ravizza takes these cases to discredit (B) as a general principle. Although the agents were not responsible for the goat's knocking over the rock or the action of the second assassin, their non-responsibility does not carry over to the respective outcomes. Because he believes that these examples discredit (B) as a general principle, Ravizza thinks that the incompatibilist belief in the non-transfer of responsibility "has been shown to be little more than an opinion in search of justification" (1994, 85) and that "incompatibilists cannot simply insist that causal determinism undermines responsibility without begging the very question they hoped to settle" (1994, 86).

I think that those philosophers who have been greatly impressed by Frankfurt-examples have been enamored by a clever metaphilosophical maneuver. In his example, Frankfurt has refocused the debate between the incompatibilists and the compatibilists so that the compatibilist perspective becomes what I have called *normal philosophy*. Frankfurt gets readers to think about freedom and responsibility from an everyday viewpoint within which we assume that persons typically are free and respon-

sible. From this everyday perspective, we simply do not entertain the
theoretical worry that determinism by itself may eliminate responsibility. We assume that Jones is responsible unless something untoward
influences him, and we do not regard the non-intervening Black (or the
goat or the second assassin in Ravizza's examples) as creating any special problem regarding responsibility. (Ravizza appears aware of this.
Note the conditional *if*: "[I]f one assassin acting alone is responsible for
the victim's death, then it would be highly implausible to think that the
fortuitous addition of another assassin should result in *neither* assassin
being even partly responsible for the death of the victim" [1994, 85].)
Thus, we are led to conclude with Frankfurt that this is a case where
alternative possibilities are not necessary and that non-responsibility does
not transfer.

The problem for Frankfurt-examples is that their persuasiveness depends on our adoption of our everyday, non-philosophical perspective,
which recognizes only unusual circumstances as challenges to our responsibility. The incompatibilist, now cast in the role of doing revolutionary
philosophy, is concerned about criticizing precisely that perspective.
Although the incompatibilist can admit that the non-intervening Black
is no *additional* problem for Jones's responsibility, the incompatibilist
insists that the question remains whether Jones is responsible in the first
place (that is, whether he lacks alternative possibilities due to determinism per se). Frankfurt's example has no resources to address that question. Frankfurt simply gets us to view the case from a perspective that
assumes that determinism is not a problem. As such, Frankfurt's example
provides no way of critiquing that assumption. The incompatibilist might
respond to Frankfurt's reversal this way: "Given that we do not know
whether Jones can be responsible if determinism is true, how can we say
whether Jones is responsible in the case where determinism is true and
Black fails to intervene?" Frankfurt's example does not address the problem that concerns the incompatibilists.

This is not to minimize the considerable cleverness of Frankfurt's move
but to analyze it. Frankfurt has gotten us to put on our compatibilistic
spectacles, and these spectacles make us myopic concerning the incompatibilist's more radical challenge. I am reminded here of Peter Unger's
(1984; 1986) analysis of the dialectic between G. E. Moore and the skeptics. According to Unger, Moore did not refute, or even speak to, the
skeptical challenge that pitches our demand for epistemic justification at
an extremely high level. Instead, by radically shifting the starting point

of his discussion from Cartesian evil demons to mundane examples such as his claim to know that he has a hand, Moore tried to move his audience to adopt our *everyday* context of epistemic justification, which would make the skeptic's standards seem incredible. But, as Unger notes, the fact that we can be worked into a position that endorses one standard gives no reason to think that we cannot view things from a conflicting perspective that endorses a different standard. The same thing holds regarding the perspectives adopted by the incompatibilists and the compatibilists.

This issue, especially given Ravizza's suggestion that (B) of the consequence argument is question-begging, proves to be very similar to the burden-of-proof problem examined in the last chapter: Does the compatibilist's or the incompatibilist's position enjoy a prima facie plausibility that places the burden of proof on the other side to disprove it? Both van Inwagen and Frankfurt have intuitions that support their side. But which side needs to prove its argument? I have argued that burden-of-proof questions are rationally unanswerable; regarding the Frankfurt case, our metaphilosophy can contribute to the answer we propose. Let me show how this might happen.

First, suppose we say that our feelings about Frankfurt's example depend on whether we wish to put on our compatibilist glasses, as Frankfurt wants us to do. If we think that this is all it amounts to—perhaps because we think that philosophers' rarified examples are a exotic Conversational genre—then we are unlikely to think that Frankfurt's example settles anything. Our attitude will be that of mild amusement. If this is the strongest metaphilosophical motivation that we bring to the example, we will treat the example with relativistic insouciance, and perhaps generalize to the conclusion that the debate between the compatibilists and incompatibilists is uninteresting.

A second metaphilosophy is more congenial to Frankfurt's maneuver. Suppose we hold that *free* is a humble term in ordinary language that we learn to wield much as we do any other abstract term. If we wish to ask whether someone would be free in a specialized context such as the incompatibilist's worry about determinism, a programmatic strategy would be to design examples that bridge the gap between our everyday context and that specialized context. In this way we would follow the sound general practice of extrapolating from our knowledge base of central cases to less central cases.

But, this strategy continues, it is only commonsensical to think that persons are not made unfree by the counterfactual power of a non-intervening controller who does not actually interfere with our choices. What better evidence could we want, then, that determinism, which by hypothesis does not *disrupt* our choices, does not by itself make us unfree? Assuming that common sense is reliable for the everyday case, its verdict should be reliable for the sort of extrapolation that Frankfurt makes. So Frankfurt's argument gains support because it extrapolates to a less certain domain from a domain where common sense yields unequivocal answers. Philosophy as Underpinning Common Sense endorses both the primacy of common sense in its own area and the careful use of common sense to answer philosophical questions.

Third, if we wish to criticize Frankfurt-examples, we could do so as rehearsed above by adopting the perspective of Philosophy as Worldview Construction and claim that the Frankfurt-examples are question-begging. This would not be easy to do, because we would have to denounce a verdict of common sense even within its own domain. We would grant no prima facie plausibility to the commonsensical view that persons are free in paradigm cases where we teach the meaning of *free* and, therefore, would refuse to extrapolate from commonsense cases to philosophically problematic ones.

It is psychologically difficult to take this third line, despite its dialectical force, because few of us wish to represent ourselves as extreme and unyielding. Some of this distaste falls under the psychological rubric of *the Rule of Reciprocity*. It is a better strategy, for example, for fund-raisers to ask for a large donation, knowing they will be turned down, and then ask for a smaller donation than to ask for the smaller donation straight off (Zimbardo and Leippe, 1991, 76–79). For the same reason, I believe, it is difficult to maintain the skeptical view that common sense has *no* epistemic worth even on its own turf. Afterall, most of us prefer to think of ourselves as reasonable persons who are willing to compromise rather than boorishly demand that we are 100 percent right. In effect, we often compromise for the sake of compromising, not because we believe that the views of the other side have merit. Nonetheless, the third line is a perfectly satisfactory rejoinder to Frankfurt's example.

4. Is Equal Proof Needed in All Areas of Philosophy?

In the *Nicomachean Ethics* (1094b, 12–15) Aristotle claims that we should demand only as much precision in a philosophical discussion as is appropriate for the subject, thereby endorsing a sliding scale of rigor for different areas of philosophy. Against Aristotle's view, philosophers with reductionist and eliminative predilections argue that all philosophical claims must meet common standards of acceptability. In different ways metaphysicians and anti-metaphysicians as diverse as Berkeley, Hume, Bertrand Russell, A. J. Ayer, Wilfrid Sellars, W. V. O. Quine, J. L. Mackie, and Gilbert Harman have demanded equal degrees of proof across different philosophical domains and drawn the negative conclusion that claims from one area that fail to meet common standards should be rejected.

Thomas Nagel's wide-ranging work exemplifies Aristotle's variable scale. Consider Nagel's treatment of the metaphysics of personhood. In "Brain Bisection and the Unity of Consciousness" (1979), Nagel considers the strange behavior of persons who have undergone hemispheric commissurotomies as treatments for gran mal epilepsy and recommends a stringent criterion for the existence of *persons*. According to Nagel, for a person to exist there must always be a definite answer to the question "How many persons are there?" Nagel argues that we cannot say either that commissurotomized patients are really one or two persons, and he concludes that these patients, as well as non-commissurotomized humans, should not be counted as *persons* at all. Rather, we should say only that brains are rough centers of mental activity, and leave open the possibility that persons do not exist.

In defending the rationality of moral discourse, Nagel pitches his demands at a much lower level. Nagel emphasizes that moral reasoning is *internal* to its subject and warns us not to expect it to conform to the methodology of molecular biology or algebra (1979, 145). Ethics should not be thought suspect simply because its claims do not meet the demands we make of scientific claims. Finally, as noted in the last chapter, in criticizing the teleological intelligibility defense of the rationality of indeterministic choices, Nagel returns to stricter requirements. Nagel gives the standard objection to the idea that reasons-explanations can explain both possible outcomes of indeterminate choices. If such choices occur, we can 'explain' why A occurs (if it occurs) by citing the agent's A-reasons, and we can 'explain' why not A occurs (if it occurs) by citing the agent's not-A-reasons, but we cannot explain why someone chooses A for the A-reasons or chooses not A for the not-A-reasons (1986, 115–16).

J. R. Lucas, who also addresses a wide range of topics, adopts Aristotle's sliding scale for normative matters. Lucas displays his easy demands regarding ethics and free will in his acceptance of a metaphysical interpretation of Aristotle's claim that "acts due to ignorance . . . are involuntary only when they bring sorrow and regret in their train" (*Nicomachean Ethics*, 1110, 18–20). I call this interpretation of Aristotle's claim *metaphysical* because it holds that our responsibility for an act done at T1 can be altered by whether we feel regret for the act when we reflect on it at T2. This is different from an epistemological interpretation, where we view Aristotle's claim as a rule of thumb to the effect that a good way to *tell* whether we are responsible at T1 is by finding out whether we feel regret at T2.

Lucas acknowledges that his view of responsibility makes responsibility subject to 'Cambridge Changes,' where

> a subsequent event alters the antecedent state of affairs: my not regretting now makes me to have been responsible then. It shows that responsibility is not just a physical concept subject to the standard physical constraints of locality and temporal antecedence, but is, rather, concerned with the significance of actions and their interpretation, where it is perfectly possible for the meaning to be altered *ex post facto*. (1993, 277)

I believe that Lucas concedes too little. On Lucas's view, responsibility is not only not a *physical* thing; it is not a *non-physical* thing, either. It is not an entity of any sort. For if responsibility is an entity—whether physical, non-physical, or Platonic—then its state *at T1* logically cannot be affected by anyone's feelings of any sort at T2. (This holds even for relational states that are subject to Cambridge Changes, such as being a husband. A man who is a husband at T1, and ceases to be a husband at T2 because his wife divorces him, does not cease to be a husband at T1.) To hold that responsibility is an entity of any sort and allow that it may be influenced in the way that Lucas's interpretation of Aristotle allows would be to allow the possibility of logically contradictory states of affairs. For on these suppositions, we might be responsible for A at T1, then, due to a feeling of regret at T2, 'become' *not* responsible for A at T1.

Rather than saying that *responsibility* is not a scientific concept, we must say that *responsibility* is not a concept for any entity whatever. This entails giving up talking about responsibility as a state of persons that might warrant the ascription of reactive attitudes, praise and blame, punishment and reward. Instead, if we go Lucas's route, we must say that there is only responsibility-discourse, which may be justifiable on various grounds but cannot be justified on the grounds that it accurately describes a real, non-linguistic feature of the world. The way that Lucas has elected to talk about responsibility makes real responsibility as the referent of responsibility-discourse impossible.

Thus, if we adopt Lucas's view of responsibility, we must not see ourselves as doing ontology. We will not be able to justify the existence of responsibility from the perspective of Philosophy as Worldview Construction, but we may be able to justify *responsibility-discourse* by appealing to an alternative metaphilosophy. If we think that the practice of ascribing responsibility is of overriding practical and moral importance, irrespective of the fact that our rules of ascription make responsibility metaphysically impossible, Philosophy as Praxis will do the job. If we think that philosophy is Conversation, it will be difficult to see why worries about the metaphysics of responsibility should pose a problem for responsibility-discourse.

The examples of Nagel and Lucas show how philosophers can adopt various criteria of rigor in different philosophical domains. The justification of such a sliding scale cannot be settled by any amount of work on the specific philosophical problems, because our theorizing at that level does not speak to the issue. Any justification we provide will have to come from the 'meta-level' by way of our metaphilosophical views about what philosophy is for and our prior decisions about what types of philosophical theories we wish to support.

5. Standard and Non-Standard Views of Moral Responsibility

Most free will theorists hold that being morally responsible for an act we perform logically requires free choice in either the incompatibilist or compatibilist form. I think that this claim is widely enough endorsed to be called the *standard view*. I have expressed the standard view with the definition of *free choice* that I am using in this book: A choice is free just in case we are morally responsible for the action that it directly produces unless there is some special reason to absolve us of responsibility.

For one who accepts the standard view, there is always a tension between *modus ponens* and *modus tollens* strategies. As noted in the last chapter, free will realists may offer the *modus ponens* argument that because we are morally responsible, we are free. Hard determinists argue via *modus tollens* that because we lack freedom we are not morally responsible. Even those who adopt the *modus ponens* version are logically committed to rebutting the *modus tollens* charge, because they accept the standard view's idea of the connection between freedom and responsibility. If we assume this connection, responsibility stands in jeopardy of disproof by a metaphysical argument that denies our freedom.

Non-standard views of responsibility are possible, however. Peter French, following J. L. Austin, offers a strategy that may be interpreted as a way of establishing responsibility that does not allow that responsibility stands in risk of a *modus tollens* disproof. According to French, we can settle the responsibility question, either positively or negatively, without speaking to the freedom question at all. We need simply to attend to our evaluation of excuses:

> [W]e seldom ask whether someone's actions were free; rather, if we are interested in assigning responsibility to him or her, we ask whether the actions were accidental, under duress, etc. If an excuse is not supportable, we hold that person accountable and regard his or her actions as having been done freely. If this analysis is correct, then determinations of responsibility precede matters of freedom. If we hold Mary responsible, then she acted freely, and we hold her responsible not because she acted freely, but because she cannot show she acted unfreely in a relevant sense, e.g., that what happened was accidental or inadvertent, etc. (1991, 21)

There are two interpretations of French's quote that correspond to the two ways of interpreting Aristotle's remarks on using regret as an indicator of responsibility for previous actions. A minimal reading would be that evaluating excuses is a reliable epistemic means for *telling whether* persons are free enough to be responsible. On this view, we would follow this algorithm: "(1) Ask: 'Shall we accept this excuse?' (2) If 'yes,' then not free. Then not responsible. (3) If 'no,' then free. Then responsible." Following this procedure would not commit us to rejecting the standard view's claim that responsibility logically implies free will. It would simply recommend an epistemic rule of thumb for finding out about free will, which leaves intact the possibility of a *modus tollens* refutation of responsibility. Hence, the minimal reading would not make French's Austinean view a competitor to the standard view.

A second interpretation would. A stronger and more natural way of reading French's claim is as a proposal for evaluating excuses on moral grounds *while holding in abeyance the question of whether the actions in question were free or not*. On this way of treating responsibility, freedom becomes parasitic upon responsibility instead of a necessary condition for it: "(1) Ask: 'Shall we accept this excuse?' (2) If 'yes,' then not morally responsible. (3) If 'no,' then morally responsible." If we adopt this algorithm we would invalidate the *modus tollens* challenge that is implicit in the standard view, because the question of responsibility would be decided by evaluating excuses. Freedom, on this interpretation, becomes an afterthought we say about choices once we have decided whether persons are responsible for them. This would be a genuine competitor to the standard view.

To the proponent of the standard view, French's Austinean proposal interpreted in the second way is obscurant and heartless. Regarding the former charge, the advocate of the standard view complains that because freedom is something we either possess or lack, it is an evasion to suggest that we can accurately determine whether someone is responsible by examining excuses without considering the general metaphysical problem of freedom. Freedom either is or is not, and we need to make our best possible estimate of which is the case, granting that we cannot be certain that we have gotten the correct answer. We cannot obviate the ontological question of free will by ignoring it. Regarding the latter charge, the defender of the standard view thinks that the second algorithm is unfair to those persons whose excuses we reject in everyday contexts. This algorithm denies such persons recourse to the plea that unless we enjoy free will, none of us are morally responsible, even if we lack specific excuses that would exonerate us in an everyday context.

How might French reply? I doubt that French can answer very forcefully if he believes that being free is a metaphysical state that one might have or fail to have and if he sees Philosophy as Worldview Construction. In this case, we would be philosophically remiss to ignore challenges to it. Psychologically, we probably would feel uncomfortable also. French, thus, would be pushed back into the weaker, epistemic interpretation. French's view interpreted in the stronger way is much more attractive, however, if we do not think that the question of whether persons are free is a metaphysical one or if we are not above all things concerned with Worldview Construction.

If we see freedom as a conventional, maybe pragmatic, maybe even literary characteristic that we impute to persons whom we decide to treat as responsible (recall Dennett's *intentional stance*), then the above complaint from those who accept the standard view will be blocked. There will be no logical room for the incompatibilist's global worry that we may all be unfree even if we have no local excuses for our actions. The view of freedom as conventional is consistent with the view that moral responsibility, too, is a conventional characteristic whose existence is coextensive with and dependent on our ascriptions of responsibility. French suggests this view when he equates responsibility with being held responsible: "Imagine a world without responsibility, a world in which no one is ever held legally or morally responsible for anything that happens" (1991, 1). On this assumption about the nature of responsibility and freedom, French's Austinean approach is exactly the one we should take.

We could also use alternative metaphilosophies to support the nonstandard view. If we think that the point of talking about responsibility and free will is to help produce morally conscientious persons, as Praxis metaphilosophy holds, then we might want to dismiss the very idea of treating free will as the standard view does. Less starkly, the Praxis view permits latitude in our thinking about free will. When our interests are *purely* theoretical, we might allow ourselves to consider the metaphysical conception of free will. But when we are concerned with the practical matter of responsibility, we *must not* allow a metaphysical worry such as that posed by the standard view's *modus tollens* challenge to bother us. We also could reach such a conclusion from the viewpoints of Philosophy as Conversation and Philosophy as Underpinning Common Sense, or from mixing these with Praxis. Worrying about the metaphysics of responsibility can be dismissed because it is a language game with conversational demerits (Philosophy as Conversation), because it doubts something that common sense knows exists—freedom (Philosophy as Underpinning Common Sense)—and because it threatens a concept we need for morality (Philosophy as Praxis).

6. Conclusion

This chapter completes my argument that many fundamental debates over free will depend on meta-level views concerning philosophy. I hope that by using this framework readers will be able to think of other illustrations besides those I have cited in the last two chapters. I do not deny that a great deal of debate occurs between disputants for whom differences in metaphilosophy are negligible. But enough of the crucial debate is rooted in meta-level differences to support the thesis that consensus will not be forthcoming. In the rest of this book I make the case for free will subjectivism by showing how the free will problem looks to a philosopher who accepts Philosophy as Continuous with Science.

II

FREE WILL FROM THE
PERSPECTIVE OF PHILOSOPHY
AS CONTINUOUS WITH SCIENCE

6

How to Frame
the Free Will Problem

This chapter provides the groundwork for the argument of part II of this book. When viewed from the species of Philosophy as Worldview Construction that I call *Philosophy as Continuous with Science*, *FREE will* is seen as an unprincipled, subjective term that cannot denote a class of objective entities. If we try to view *free choices* as denoting a class of choices whose freeness is a characteristic of the choices themselves, it becomes logically contradictory. If *free choice* is not contradictory, its meaning fragments into a multiplicity of subjective senses. This also would prevent the term from denoting a unified objective reference class, inasmuch as the term would denote wildly disparate entities for different speakers.

In section 1, I propose to frame the free will problem in a radically non-question-begging way. The trichotomy of hard determinism/soft determinism/libertarianism and the dichotomy of incompatibilism vs. compatibilism need to be replaced by a framework that includes more possibilities and does not presuppose that the free will problem is a real problem. In section 2, I show that distinguishing between the positive and negative claims of traditional incompatibilists and compatibilists yields a taxonomy of four possible positions rather than just two. In section 3, I show how looking at the claims of the incompatibilists and compatibilists from the previous section in a slightly different way produces a fifth theory that entails that the concept *free will*, when taken to have objective reference, is logically incoherent.

1. A Radical Approach to Free Will

Many philosophers—including probably more who do not specialize in
the area of free will than those who do—suspect that there is something
fundamentally wrong with the free will problem. Perhaps none of the
traditional answers are acceptable because there is something wrong with
the question. I knew of no other development of this view when I wrote
The Non-Reality of Free Will, although I learned later that a view similar
to mine had been sketched by Peter Unger (1984). Interestingly, even in
the heyday of Logical Positivism, when one metaphysical problem after
another was denounced as a pseudo-problem, the most influential posi-
tivist treatments of free will (those of Moritz Schlick and A. J. Ayer) were
compatibilistic ones fully in the tradition of Hobbes and Hume. But to
anyone truly suspicious of the free will question, compatibilism is, as they
used to say, not part of the solution but part of the problem. A more radical approach that questions the meaning and possible reference of *free
will* (and *free choice*) is needed if we are to address the suspicion that
there is something wrong with the entire problem.

To approach the free will issue in a radical way we need to view free
will skeptically. This means seeing free will as a posit that needs justification, just like any other candidate for admission to our ontology. The
existence of free will is not to be justified phenomenologically, because
it is possible that our 'awareness' of freedom is produced by nefarious
agents who also select our choices for us, as in Richard Taylor's ingenious physiologist (1974, 50) and Daniel Dennett's (1984) hypnotists and
puppeteers. Our choices are not to be deemed free by appeal to commonly
accepted criteria (Flew, 1959), because the radical approach questions
whether those commonsense criteria are correct. We are not employing
Philosophy as Underpinning Common Sense. Our choices are not to be
judged free on the grounds that such a belief is valuable to our moral
pursuits, because our radical view does not endorse Philosophy as Praxis.
In sum, we beg the question against the philosopher with radical worries
about free will if we award free will any initial plausibility by using any
of the liberal intermediate philosophical principles or any metaphilosophy
other than Philosophy as Worldview Construction.

The radical approach that I employ acquires its distinctive character
from its acceptance of intermediate philosophical principles endorsing
skeptical epistemic standards, a realist interpretation of theories, restric-
tive scruples on ontological postulations, strong demands on explana-

tion, and Hume's principle. These intermediate principles constitute much of the vision of the philosopher who tries to complete the worldview given by science without straying from the parsimonious methodology of inference to the best explanation that enables science to achieve its successes. This is the variety of Worldview Construction that I call *Philosophy as Continuous with Science*. The argument I begin in this chapter is based on my announced metaphilosophy and intermediate principles, and it tries for plausibility relative to those premises. According to the central thesis of this book, arguments such as mine will not move someone who holds different meta-level views.

2. Four Free Will Theories

Understanding *free choices* as I did in chapter 1 as whatever sort of choices are sufficient to make us morally responsible for the actions those choices produce, we need to ask about its possible reference. We can derive four theories from the claims of traditional incompatibilists and compatibilists if we distinguish between idealized, non-equivalent positive and negative theses of each:

> (IN) *Incompatibilism's Negative Claim*: "Determined choices cannot be free."
> (IP) *Incompatibilism's Positive Claim*: "Indeterminacy (suitably located) within our choice-making process gives rise to free choice."
> (CN) *Compatibilism's Negative Claim*: "Undetermined choices cannot be free."
> (CP) *Compatibilism's Positive Claim*: "Under certain conditions, determined choices can be free."

(IN) is the clearest of the four statements, given its simplicity: If a choice is determined, then it is unfree. (*Determined* must be understood to mean *causally determined by events other than the agent's own earlier undetermined free choice* if we are to handle views such as Robert Kane's [1996] that hold that an agent's undetermined free choice at T1 can determine a subsequent free choice by that agent at T2.) Those who accept (IN) find it quite obvious. Incompatibilist thought-experiments such as those involving nefarious neurosurgeons and cosmic puppeteers are used not to *prove* (IN) but to illustrate it (Dennett, 1984, chapter 1).

If my earlier analysis of Peter van Inwagen's consequence argument is correct, that argument does not *prove* (IN) but relies on our pro-(IN) intuitions. (IP) is less compelling than (IN), even to libertarians, because it raises the enduring difficulty of specifying exactly how indeterminacy contributes to making choices free. (CN) is not as striking as (IN) on first reading, because it seems to be an inductive generalization without the dramatic examples that one can give to support (IN). It gains plausibility, though, when read as a challenge: "Any place you incompatibilists try to locate indeterminacy within human choices, we compatibilists can show that it *decreases* rather than *increases* the freedom of those choices." Finally, (CP) is also imprecise, awaiting specific proposals by compatibilists. I believe that these proposals have become increasingly attractive as compatibilists have refined their versions of that theory in the last twenty years.

Consider next the logical relations that hold between these four theses on the assumption (which I reject in the next section) that *free choice*, defined in terms of moral responsibility, is a logically coherent concept. The incompatibilists' claims (IN) and (IP) are logically consistent, though non-equivalent; the compatibilists' claims (CN) and (CP) are also consistent though non-equivalent. There are two pairs of contradictories— the negative and the positive claims of the respective theorists ([IN] contradicts [CP], and [IP] contradicts [CN]). Since there are four statements, each of which may be viewed as being true or false, there are sixteen mathematically possible results; but given our assumption about the contradictories, we can extract only four different theories:

	(IN)	*(IP)*	*(CN)*	*(CP)*
Classical Incompatibilism	True	True	False	False
Classical Compatibilism	False	False	True	True
No-Free-Will-Either-Way Theory	True	False	True	False
Free-Will-Either-Way Theory	False	True	False	True

Even if we prefer Classical Incompatibilism or Classical Compatibilism, we have to admit the conceptual possibility of the latter two theories. These need to be distinguished and, if we wish to be comprehensive, evaluated. (Peter Strawson calls the third theory "moral skepticism" in his 1962 article, but he does not examine it there. I know of no previous recognition of the fourth theory.) If we try to assess each of the four theories predicated on (IN), (IP), (CN), and (CP) while holding in check as much as we can our commitments to the classical views, we may find that the latter two candidates have significant appeal. For hard-minded thinkers, this might seem especially true for the No-Free-Will-Either-Way Theory, because the strength of both incompatibilism and compatibilism may seem to lie in their negative claims, not their positive accounts. This may be an important reason why the free will debate seems to admit of so little progress: Each side invokes strong intuitions that reject the theory of the other side without being able to generate correspondingly strong intuitions for their positive theses. (In politics this is called 'negative campaigning.') On the other hand, some of the more tender-hearted may be moved toward the Free-Will-Either-Way Theory once that view is presented as a logical possibility. The point to notice is that playing by the usual rules provides four theories to evaluate instead of only two. And if we add to the options of rejecting and accepting the four principles the alternative of being agnostic about them, we would arrive at an even larger taxonomy. (See Alfred Mele's *Autonomous Agents* for a view that is close to the Free-Will-Either-Way Theory but is agnostic about [IN].)

3. Another Theory

Consider what happens if we break one of the rules in evaluating the positive and negative claims of Classical Incompatibilism and Classical Compatibilism. Suppose we set aside the assumption that the pair (IN) and (CP) and the pair (IP) and (CN) are contradictories and instead try to evaluate each statement on its own merits. I emphasize again that I define *free choice* throughout this book in terms of justifying moral responsibility. It will not suffice to criticize my argument simply to assert that I have forgotten that *free choice* is ambiguous. I know it is, but my claims about (IN), (IP), (CN), and (CP) are meant to hold for the one, univocal sense of *free choice* that I have stipulated.

I often feel inclined to accept (IN) and (CN). Incompatibilists seem correct to disparage the responsibility-justifying freedom of determined choices (which could not have been different categorically than they were), and the compatibilist complaint that locating indeterminacy within our choice-making process would reduce such freedom seems correct also. Together these two claims entail that determinism would destroy our responsibility-justifying freedom and indeterminism would make things even worse. Nonetheless, I do not always find that the pessimism generated by my acceptance of (IN) and (CN) carries over to my evaluation of (IP) and (CP). Sometimes I feel no hesitation in assenting to the positive accounts (IP) and (CP), even while I assent to their apparent contradictories (IN) and (CN).

By accepting all four statements, I seem to have done something logically odd. Have I? The *rejection* of all candidates is not always remarkable in philosophical disputes. For instance, there is a tradition in normative ethics of rejecting every normative theory that comes along, without thinking that the enterprise of finding a best or true normative account is thereby undercut. Such ethicists view their endeavor as forever trying to approximate a best account. It's just that ethics is difficult, they tell us. Real havoc occurs, though, when theorists *affirm* conflicting theories. Imagine what it would be like to say that Kantian and utilitarian theories are both true, instead of saying that they are both false. If we can show that these *apparently* contradictory theories are 'equally true,' then we have undone normative ethics altogether. The only way that both of these theories could be 'true' is if moral truth were relativized to individuals or groups of individuals, which is to say that they are not objectively true at all. By analogy, by accepting all four statements from the incompatibilists and compatibilists, I have claimed that *free choice* in the moral-responsibility-justifying sense can have no objective reference, that freeness can exist only in the eye of the beholder.

There seem to be just two things that we could say about my acceptance of (IN), (IP), (CN), and (CP). Either *free choice* in the stipulated sense is logically coherent, in which case I have contradicted myself. Or I am not guilty of contradicting myself, in which case *free choice* in the stipulated sense, *if* taken to have objective reference, is logically incoherent. I believe that the second alternative is the case.

This much stated, I need to address the logical coherence of accepting (IN), (IP), (CN), and (CP) all at once. I shall not countenance the rebuttal that I *must* be contradicting myself because we know that *free choice* is coherent; that would be question-begging. Now, it may look as if I am setting up the dispute so that it will come out to be a draw. In the long run, if philosophy is what I think it is, the outcome probably *is* a draw. But within the short run—namely, part II of this book, where I presuppose Philosophy as Continuous with Science—a draw is not in order. Rather, I think that on my preferred metaphilosophy the second alternative is more attractive than the claim that I have contradicted myself. To begin the argument let us ask whether there *could* be some objective fact that would show that my acceptance of all four statements at once is in error.

I am not asking the psychological question of whether some objective fact could ever force me to admit that I have contradicted myself—I am not trying to turn dogmatism into a virtue. Nor am I asking the epistemological question whether some objective fact could ever *prove* that I am wrong. Even if the answer to this question is negative, that would not prove my thesis. Rather, I am asking the metaphysical question whether an objective fact could exist that would make my position wrong, regardless of whether I would ever accept that fact or whether it could prove me wrong. What would reality have to be like to make it true that I am contradicting myself by accepting all four statements? If there could not be such a fact about the nature of reality that would make it the case that I have contradicted myself, then I have not. I begin by examining a case that I use as a model for viewing the two sides of the disagreement about *free choice*.

If we ask several persons what qualities make a person a jerk and who the jerks in the world are, we will get different answers. (*Jerk*, in Americanese, is a pejorative term for persons.) Different persons will use different criteria, so probably there will be no two persons whose non-null extension of the term will be the same. Worse, depending on the frame of mind we are in when we decide that someone is a jerk, sometimes we will decide that a person is a jerk and a moment later decide the person is not a jerk, without receiving any new information about the person.

Philosophically, we might take an objectivist or subjectivist view of the existence of jerks. An objectivist would say that there are correct answers to what makes someone a jerk and who the jerks are, whether anyone actually knows the answers or not. The problem is simply that it is very difficult to know the right answers. A subjectivist would say that the conflicting way that the term *jerk* is applied gives strong reason to think that there cannot be an objectively correct answer. According to this view, *jerk* is a paradigmatic emotive word, and we would be foolish to try to make room in our ontology for jerks as an real class of entities. What exists, according to the subjectivist, are persons whom other persons view with displeasure at various times. Persons are admitted as good ontological candidates. So are persons' psychological states of disliking other persons. But according to the subjectivist, there is no objective class of persons who *are* jerks in virtue possessing an objective (not necessarily Platonic) characteristic of 'jerkiness' or 'jerkhood.'

The subjectivist's claim that when applying the title *jerk* conflicting opinions are equally correct is equivalent to saying that it is logically impossible for there to *be* jerks, again understood as a class of persons who have the objective characteristic of being a jerk. Emphasizing the ontological question and not shying away from what might sound odd, we can say that although there are persons whom other persons call *jerks*, there really *can be* no such thing as a jerk. The 'quality' of being a jerk 'resides' only in the subjective attitudes of persons who respond favorably toward the various objective features of the persons.

Free choice, in my view, is analogous to *jerk*. Our acceptance of (IN), (IP), (CN), and (CP) depends on our vacillating ideas about what makes our choices 'good enough' to justify moral responsibility. The way we pose the question affects the answers we reach. To ask whether *determined* choices can be free poses the question in such a way as to ask whether a choice can be good enough to count as free if we theoretically can trace its causes back to the laws of nature and events that occurred before the chooser was born (as in van Inwagen's consequence argument). When we frame the question in this historical way, it is very tempting to assign determined choices a negative grade. When we assign this grade, we affirm (IN). To ask whether an *undetermined* choice can be free is to frame matters so that we focus on the perils of indeterminacy, bringing to mind examples of unpredictable happenings that are not under the control of the chooser. When we are impressed that such cases would reduce our freedom and responsibility, we assent to (CN).

Nonetheless, having assented to (IN) and (CN), there is no reason—beyond self-imposed constraints that we might *think* are logical constraints—why we cannot give the high marks to certain choices that are implicit in (CP) and (IP). (By assenting to [IP] and [CP] as well as [IN] and [CN], I distinguish my subjectivist view from the objectivist No-Free-Will-Either-Way Theory.) When I think about (CP), I find that I focus on the internal rationality of choices. When I do, the fact that the choices are determined and, hence, theoretically predictable since before the chooser was even born strikes me as irrelevant to their responsibility-justifying freedom. In doing so, I affirm (CP). Finally, if we bring a different mind-set to the issue and 'lighten up' (as Dan Quayle advised Al Gore to do on television during the 1992 campaign) and do not demand that free choices be so rigidly connected to what went before, then we have no difficulty in giving up the claim that undetermined choices are unfree. This is to accept (IP).

On the view that I am advancing, the judgments we make about the freedom of choices are not made true or false by facts about the choices themselves. The freeness of choices is not even a characteristic that could exist in the choices; all that the freeness of choices amounts to is the question of how we feel about or 'grade' choices. The grades we give do not track a characteristic that choices may have or fail to have; instead, those grades depend on our opinions and feelings about the actual characteristics of choices. Our opinions and feelings on this score are moved by a disorganized variety of factors that have little to do with the choices themselves. Instead they involve such subjective factors as the way we frame the questions, our personal histories, our temperaments, our philosophical biases, and our ideologies, as well as other idiosyncratic elements. Also relevant in our judgments concerning the goodness of choices are the competing exemplars of freedom that philosophers have un-self-consciously constructed throughout the free will debate (Double, 1991B, chapter 5). Taken together, these considerations, and doubtless others, explain why we *do* affirm (IN), (IP), (CN), and (CP). This explanation creates a strong case for thinking that we are *correct* to do so.

If we take *free* to denote a characteristic of choices themselves, that characteristic is contradictory. A free choice in the sense that justifies moral responsibility may be determined (CP) and cannot be determined (IN), can be undetermined (IP) and cannot be undetermined (CN). Such a 'characteristic' cannot belong to a choice itself any more than one person can both be and not be a jerk at the same time. Since the 'freeness' of choices themselves is a logically impossible characteristic, it cannot exist. We are forced, therefore, to understand talk about the freeness of choices in a subjectivized way. Philosophers may assign specific, coherent senses to *free* in their own idiolects, just as each of us may do with *jerk*. They may then inquire about free choices in those senses, such as whether that sort of freedom is compatible with determinism and so on. (I owe this to one of the readers.) Nonetheless, the fact that we can specify various definitions for *free choice* is irrelevant to the problem I pose: that in its moral-responsibility-justifying sense, *free choice* has no chance of denoting a unified class of choices that are themselves free. Here is why that maneuver will not help the objectivist.

Suppose that E is an evaluative term that purports to pick out a class of entities possessing some evaluative characteristic. Then to assign an individual A to that class (to say that A is E) is to evaluate A. But suppose that there are no evaluative truths. Then there will be no truths concerning whether we have correctly assigned individual A to class E.

Now apply this line of reasoning to free choice. I argue in the next two chapters that *free will* and *moral responsibility* are moral terms. I also endorse the more obvious premise that to claim that choices of a certain sort make us morally responsible for our behavior is to make a moral claim. Add to this the subjectivist premise that there are no moral truths. It follows from these claims that there can be no truth to the matter of whether the compatibilists or incompatibilists have made the 'correct' decision concerning free will and moral responsibility. This would be parallel to the subjectivist's saying that there can be no objectively correct decision to make as to who the jerks are. If moral non-realism is correct, then there could be no answer to what kind of free will is "worth wanting," to use Dennett's expression, given that free will realists are making moral claims.

4. Conclusion

By providing the analogy between *jerk* and *free choice* I illustrate two mutually supporting, but independent, reasons for thinking that there can be no objective class of moral-responsibility-justifying free choices, at least for thinkers who accept my meta-level views. The first reason is that *free choice* is evaluative. To call a choice *free*—in the sense that is connected to moral responsibility—is to morally grade the choice. Thus, if there can be no objective moral truths, there cannot be objectively free choices. In chapters 8 and 9 I develop the argument that *free choice* is a moral concept and show how that fact supports free will subjectivism. The second reason is that *free choice* fragments into several equally good but conflicting senses, just as there are many conflicting criteria we may assign to *jerk*. I contend that such fragmentation, irrespective of the moral nature of *free choice*, would show that the freeness of choices is not a characteristic of an objective class of choices. In the next chapter I show that *free choice* fragments and demonstrate how this counts against the existence of free will.

7

The Fragmentation
of Free Will

In the last chapter I sketched the argument that *free will* in the sense that is supposed to justify moral responsibility is a term that has only subjectivist reference that skews from speaker to speaker. Just as there is no 'right answer' to the question of who the jerks are, there is no right answer to whether this kind of free will is compatible or incompatible with determinism. The four statements that constitute the prototypical positive and negative claims of the incompatibilists and compatibilists are equally 'true,' despite the fact that they appear to logically conflict. This is to say that there is no answer to the question of whether determined choices can be free. Consequently, there can be no answer to the question of whether Classical Incompatibilism, Classical Compatibilism, the No-Free-Will-Either-Way Theory, or the Free-Will-Either-Way Theory is correct. The reason there is no truth to the matter is that *free will*, defined in terms of moral responsibility, is a logically incoherent term that cannot denote a unified class of real entities outside of the subjective predilections of users of the term.

In this chapter I support that argument by answering two types of objections: (1) that free will does not really fragment into the varieties given in the last chapter, and (2) that even if fragmentation does occur, fragmentation does not prove my non-realist conclusion. The latter objection, which has been expressed by several critics of *The Non-Reality of Free Will*, will receive most of my attention in this chapter. In section 1, I examine what I call the *unity objection* and give my reply. In section 2, I sketch the *fragmentation-is-no-problem objection*. In sections 3 through 5, I address the latter challenge, especially the one posed by David

Cockburn. In section 6, I examine the version of the fragmentation-is-no-problem objection provided by Alfred Mele.

1. The Unity Objection

Remembering that there are types of freedom that all sides agree are *not* relevant to the free will problem and may be set aside, one way to resist my subjectivist argument is to claim that there is a correct account of moral-responsibility-justifying free choices that settles the question of whether a *free* choice can be determined, no matter how unsure we are about the account. I call this the *unity objection*. According to this objection, the free will that is needed for moral responsibility does not really divide into compatibilist and incompatibilist varieties. Why not distinguish between the epistemological issue concerning our lack of knowledge of which account is correct and the ontological issue of whether there is a correct account? As Mark Bernstein suggests (in correspondence), the fact that a penny appears to have different shapes when viewed from different perspectives scarcely proves that the penny does not have a single shape. Even if the task of finding out the true account of *free choice* is perennially baffling, objectivism may be true so long as there is a single correct notion of *free choice* that denotes free choices and would settle the debate between the incompatibilists and compatibilists if we could recognize it were we to find it.

I believe that we should reject the unity objection for two reasons. I grant that these reasons do not absolutely prove that *free choice* fragments, but I think that they are very strong reasons relative to Philosophy as Continuous with Science. First, when the unity position is viewed solely in terms of the evidence for it, it is not very plausible. As illustrated in *The Non-Reality of Free Will* (chapter 5), there are many cases where we would say both "S chooses freely" and "S chooses unfreely," depending on the point of view we take when we make the judgments. These are not borderline cases where we have blurred intuitions, but cases where we would say definitely "yes" and definitely "no." The conviction that underneath our jumbled assessments there *must* be a metaphysical unity concerning the conditions under which persons choose freely is perhaps Platonistic (recall Wittgenstein on games and tools) and is, in any event, question-begging. This is not to say that it is *impossible* that there is a deep unity that underlies responsibility-justifying free choices, but only that the evidence we have supports the fragmentation thesis.

The postulation of unity cannot be justified as the best explanation of our mixed and conflicting intuitions about whether determinism makes us unfree in the moral-responsibility-justifying sense. Therefore, if we do reach that conclusion, it must be justified in some other way. This might be attempted by an appeal to a Platonistic premise that *free choice* in this sense 'must' denote a unitary class of entities or by a consideration such as Praxis or Underpinnings metaphilosophy. Because metaphilosophies are not refutable, such applications of alternative metaphilosophies would not be refutable. But we can say this: Relative to a view of philosophy that tries to keep its postulations to the minimum needed to explain what we have to admit to our ontology—that is, Philosophy as Continuous with Science—the postulation of unity appears quite weak.

A second reason for rejecting the unity objection lies at the level of intermediate philosophical principles. FREE choices, of the sort that are supposed to justify moral responsibility, and MORAL responsibility itself belong to moral theory. But according to the moral subjectivism I endorse, moral terms have no objective reference, and moral judgments are never true but at most express speakers' non-truth-valued feelings and attitudes. Hence, *free* logically cannot denote an objective quality of choices. I develop the connection between moral subjectivism and free will subjectivism in chapters 8 and 9.

2. The Fragmentation-Is-No-Problem Objection

The second challenge to my argument is to admit that there is no single, responsibility-justifying meaning of *free choice* to be found but to deny that this fact supports subjectivism. I call this the *fragmentation-is-no-problem objection*. According to this line, even if fragmentation occurs it does not support subjectivism. I shall examine two ways that this objection could be developed.

First, consider the term *bald*. Combining suggestions by Bernstein and Richard Brook (in correspondence), why not say that *bald* refers to *whatever* scarcity and distribution of hair meets any competent speaker's definition of *bald*? For instance, bald compatibilists might believe that being hirsute is compatible with having only 5,000 hairs on one's head, while bald incompatibilists might hold that having 5,000 hairs or fewer entails that one is bald. Even if there are several logically conflicting definitions of *bald*, the term retains objective reference in the idiolects of individuals. We could say a similar thing about *free* in *free choice*. As long as we can produce definitions that are not self-contradictory, the fact that other definitions contradict them need cast no doubt on the objective reference of our use of *free choice.*

David Cockburn (1992), in a review of my 1991 book, provides a second variant on the fragmentation-is-no-problem objection. Cockburn accepts the following theses: (i) Neither incompatibilism nor compatibilism involves any contradiction. (ii) Both views have significant intuitive appeal given the ways we think about free will and responsibility. (iii) There probably is no possible *philosophical* resolution of the debate between the incompatibilists and compatibilists. (iv) Free will is not a single type of entity. (v) It is false to claim that there can be no such thing as free will.

According to Cockburn, the (acknowledged) mess that philosophers get into when they try to give rational reconstructions of our thinking about freedom and responsibility does not go far toward proving the conclusion that free will cannot exist:

> It could be that when, confronted with particular examples, we are asked
> 'Is he free?,' we are pulled in different directions because we are, without
> fully realizing it, responding to a range of different questions: we first ask
> ourselves whether gratitude would be in place, then shift to the question
> of whether praise would be in place, then to the question of whether this
> individual's condition is something to which we should aspire, and so on.
> And the fact that we give different answers to these questions need reveal
> no inconsistency in our normal thought. To the extent that this is so,
> Double's conclusion that there is no answer to the dispute between com-
> patibilists and incompatibilists over the correct analysis of free will will
> be left standing: on the grounds not that there can be no such thing as free
> will, but, rather, that 'free will' is not a *single* thing. (1992, 386)

3. Two Preliminary Reasons to Reject Both Types of the Fragmentation-Is-No-Problem Objection

One preliminary point is that if my argument from moral subjectivism and the moral nature of free will to its non-existence defeats the unity response, the same argument would defeat all varieties of the fragmentation-is-no-problem response. So the latter response is equally vulnerable on that score.

A second point is that my opponent's sanguine acceptance of fragmentation shows a lack of seriousness about ontology. A metaphysical realist thinks that the point of using the referring terms of a language is to designate the entities that make up the world. Language is not a vehicle for 'creating' entities. Consider again the pejorative noun *jerk*. The whole point behind using the term is to express dislike of the designee. (This captures what used to be called the *emotive meaning* of the term.) There are, of course, countless criteria that speakers use to decide, first, who the linguistically appropriate candidates are, and, second, who the jerks are. (These criteria constitute the *descriptive meaning* of the term.) Some speakers think that an unintentional manifestation of a psychological state such as arrogance is a sufficient condition for someone's being a jerk. Others disagree, believing that an intentional display is required. Still others are more liberal, believing that some overt offense is required. Some college faculty think that all college administrators are jerks simply by virtue of being administrators. And so on.

Given these disorderly and conflicting descriptive criteria, the reference of *jerk* varies tremendously from speaker to speaker. There is no such thing as 'the' class of jerks, unless you mean the union of all the persons who anyone thinks are jerks. (This would be a problematic class, because it would contain many individuals who many speakers believe are non-jerks.) This suggests to anyone with realist proclivities that jerks just are not 'out there' in the way that cabbages and carbon atoms are. Hence, in addition to the subjectivists' worries about the reality of the evaluative realm, it seems that the fragmentation problem alone suggests that the world does not contain a real class of jerks. Rather, we should say that there exists the class of persons, and among these there are some persons who dislike some other persons, and the former sometimes call the latter *jerks*.

Mark Bernstein points out that if we apply this eliminativist argument to persons, lack of consensus would also cast doubt on the existence of persons, thereby showing that my argument proves too much. But working at the level of the present discussion, it is fair to respond that the denotation of *jerk* is far more problematic than that of *person*. If we were to survey native speakers on whether 100 subjects are examples of jerks or persons, we would find much more consensus about the latter. To me, Bernstein's objection illustrates the contextual nature of ontological discussions. In the present discussion philosophers assume the existence of persons and worry about the existence of free will. In an ontological inquiry pitched at a different level, the existence of persons might be up for grabs. In discussions of normative ethics, almost everyone assumes the existence of free will. (See Smilansky, 1994, for an interesting counter-example.) The way that philosophers selectively scrutinize specific targets while assuming that other entities are unproblematic may be defended or criticized: defended because we have to proceed that way (Neurath's boat) or criticized as self-serving.

The moral regarding the fragmentation of the reference of *jerk* is repeated with indexical terms. *This* and *here* are terms that enable us to refer to parts of reality that are of special interest to us by drawing attention to the relation between those parts of the cosmos and us. According to my view, the cosmos does not include 'thisses' and 'heres' in addition to the things that do exist.

One may object that I am being too finicky about ontological matters. What *harm* is there in saying that jerks are just as real as persons are, even if we cannot specify an objective principle for determining who the jerks and non-jerks are? We would have to say, by parity of reasoning, that thisses and heres are just as respectable entities as carbon atoms. This reply also would have to be made regarding other 'non-natural kinds': book-women (the disjunctive entities that [who] are either books or women), emeroses (things that are either emeralds prior to t or roses otherwise), and Wednesday would-be hair-raisers (events that would cause the hair on my neck to rise if and only if they occurred on Wednesdays). Well, it may be admitted that all of this sounds strange. But what, my opponent wants to know, is the *decisive* reason for saying that fragmented entities lack objective existence? A quick answer is that if we accept the ontological conservatism implicit in Philosophy as Continuous with Science, we must not let unjustified entities into our picture of what exists. In a Quinean spirit we might say that once we have admitted persons, we do not *need* jerks also. To give a more detailed answer, however, we need to examine the two variants of the fragmentation-is-no-problem response at length.

4. Reasons to Reject the *Bald* Example

I begin my examination of the *bald* example by pointing out some important disanalogies between *bald* and *free*. First, *bald* is an observational term, while *free* is a theoretical term. There are many ways to be bald, all of them recognizable by persons with no specialized knowledge. A dispute over whether a person who has a certain number and distribution of hairs is bald would be simply a disagreement over the definition of the term. A dispute over whether someone who wears a toupee is bald would also be definitional. *Free*, on the other hand, is a theoretical term in two ways. First, whether a determined person can be free is not observationally decided, but awaits the result of a perennial philosophical debate. Second, *free* is not necessary even as a theoretical term for the explanation of behavior in psychology; it is needed only when we wish to appraise the quality of behavior—whether in the law or in everyday life—and, thus, belongs to philosophy and normative theory.

Second, in disputes over the correct definition of *bald* or disputes over the correct prototypes (Smith and Medin, 1981) of baldness, little is at stake. The reason for having the word *bald* is to quantify hair in an inexact way. There is no reasonable worry that anyone's operational definition or selection of a prototype is *intellectually* or *morally* flawed. *Free* in the sense connected to moral responsibility, on the other hand, is bound up with moral questions. When philosophers ask whether S chose freely, we are asking whether, as Cockburn notes, we should feel reactive attitudes toward S, whether we may praise or blame S, and other morally loaded questions. We cannot accept operational definitions of *free* as we could with *bald*, because the concept *free* is morally loaded, and because there can be serious practical consequences for incorrectly concluding that someone is free.

The first two differences lead to a third. A disagreement between what I have called bald compatibilists and bald incompatibilists could be settled by each side saying: "Well, if what we *mean* by *bald* is *your* definition, then you are right. If what we mean by *bald* is *my* definition, then I am right. There is no serious disagreement between us about any non-linguistic fact; we differ only verbally."

Compatibilists and incompatibilists in the free will debate do not see things in this way. They do *not* say that determinism is compatible with compatibilist free will and incompatible with incompatibilist free will and leave it at that. Even Ted Honderich, who thinks that compatibilists and incompatibilists are talking about different kinds of freedom, believes that there is an objective standpoint from which we can deduce the true consequences of determinism (1993, chapters 7–10). As a popular American tabloid says, "Enquiring minds want to know." Philosophers want to know whether persons can be *truly* free if determinism is the case, not merely free according to someone's theoretically loaded definition or prototype. This is a serious matter to philosophers who believe that free will can exist. Incompatibilists make a serious, and in many cases unfair, charge against compatibilists when they claim that the latter admit that persons cannot possess deep, responsibility-enabling free will if all choices are determined: "[N]early all compatibilists . . . agree that true responsibility and true self-determination are impossible if determinism is true. That is why they standardly attempt to define freedom in such a way that it does not involve true responsibility (or true self-determination)" (G. Strawson, 1986, 27).

These three points show why the objectivist's comparison between *free* and *bald* does not hurt my fragmentation argument. *Bald* fragments, but still denotes in its fragmented senses. *Bald #1* may denote one type of baldness, *Bald #2* another type, and so on. Most adjectives are capable of this sort of fragmented reference, although perhaps not most key adjectives in philosophical discussions. Philosophers' ideas about free will, as opposed to operationally definable freedoms (e.g., freedom of speech, freedom of religion), are pinned down by free will's connection to moral questions involving desert for praise, blame, punishment, reward, and reactive attitudes, as well as human dignity and autonomy. This means that if *free will* fragments and, thus, can refer only to various types of free choices that support some but not other moral properties, then the essential thing has been lost.

The characteristic or property of being free, as used in philosophers' discussions of free will, is a theoretical posit we impute to persons' choices for the purpose of justifying the ascription of a unified package of moral properties. Free will is supposed to provide ontological warrant for the ascription of at least these: (1) reactive attitudes; (2) deserved moral praise and moral censure; (3) deserved reward and punishment; (4) a special degree of dignity that makes us participating members of moral communities (and not free riders such as sentient-but-unfree humans and non-humans); (5) a special type of autonomy or self-governance that we do not impute to non-free beings.

In ascribing free will to persons, we purport to justify the package as a whole. Each component is necessary to the justification of viewing persons as responsible persons. If those properties cannot be satisfied jointly, free will cannot exist. If neither the compatibilists nor incompatibilists are correct in thinking that their theories can support the package, then *free will* fragments into incompatibilist and compatibilist varieties, perhaps into several subspecies of each. If so, then the sort of free will that agents enjoy would support at most some, but not other, moral properties. Thus, persons could satisfy only some of the moral properties (1–5). Any concept of a free person that presupposes the conjunction of these properties would be unsatisfiable.

If fragmentation occurs, troublesome questions arise. If we cannot have all the moral properties that we prephilosophically think we have, then we must decide which is 'better'—for example, for a person to be free in the sense that legitimizes (1) and (4) or in the sense that legitimizes (2) and (5), and so on. This is unacceptable to prephilosophical common sense, which assumes that we enjoy all five. I should hope that it would be unacceptable to libertarians and compatibilists, if they see themselves as trying to *vindicate* commonsense views about freedom and responsibility rather than *surrender* them. I concede, however: Anyone who has no interest in seeing whether we can vindicate these moral properties is entitled to call choices that do not support these properties *free*. Such a thinker, though, is not worrying about what I am worrying about in the free will problem.

My argument so far depends on the premise that free will, in the sense that is supposed to justify moral responsibility, is supposed to underwrite the above conjunction of moral properties. I do not think that anyone can *prove* that premise, but I can support it. One way is to ask readers to consider my claim in light of the fact that the compatibilists and the incompatibilists think that it is so important to give the *right* account of free will. If these theorists did not believe that fragmentation would be destructive to free will, wouldn't they be more willing to compromise than they are? I have granted throughout that there are senses of *free* that have nothing to do with the free will problem (Kane, 1996, chapter 1). But having set aside the senses that are not relevant to the problem, incompatibilists and compatibilists believe that there is a central concept that needs to be *correctly* explicated.

I also can support the needed premise by providing an analogy with an argument in the split-brain literature. According to Roland Puccetti (1981, 117), the concept of a person entails that the same person is the locus of many different types of mental states coming from different modalities. If the stimulations coming into our bodies are experienced by different *subsystems*, but not by the same *person*, then there is not a person at home in the cranium:

Take any three friends and ask them to imagine being, respectively, visual cortex, auditory cortex, and a limbic center connected with a single cerebral hemisphere. Then entertain the picture of all three attending to, say, an attractive member of the opposite sex slowly disrobing to the music of bongo drums. One friend sees the dancer disrobing, but hears and feels nothing. Another friend hears the music, but sees and feels nothing. The third feels sexually aroused, but seeing and hearing nothing, hasn't a clue why. This is absurd, yet it is the committee model of mentality. I for one know it does not model *my* mind, for in the imaginative exercise *I* would be seeing, hearing, and feeling aroused. (1981, 177)

Similarly, I think that the ascription of freedom to our choices must justify the unified ascription of the whole package of moral properties given in (1–5), on pain of there not being a *free* agent at all. On my view, one and the same person warrants reactive attitudes, deserves expressed praise or blame, deserves reward or punishment, possesses a special degree of dignity not shared by unfree beings, and is autonomous. Cockburn suggests that in special cases we may feel that certain moral properties separate from each other. Cockburn thinks, for example, that moral saints should be emulated but not praised, because it would be odd to praise persons whose good characters were so set that they could not have acted badly (1992, 386). On this point, I believe that Cockburn conflates the distinct notions of *deserving praise* and the *pragmatic oddness of praising saints*. But even if we grant Cockburn's point, special cases do not count against my claim that typically we demand that the entire package will be instantiated, any more than admitting that a split-brain patient sometimes lacks a fully integrated consciousness shows that the concept of a person does not entail unified consciousness in the normal case.

Although my list of five moral properties is given in philosophical language, I believe (but confess that I have no resources to show) that most lay persons would agree that all five elements are essential to our commonsense view of persons as *responsible*. It is this prephilosophical idea of responsibility, which I think is not a philosophers' fiction, that philosophers try to capture with their accounts of free will. Some philosophers would go so far as to say that all five are essential to our viewing persons as *persons*. I believe that there can be wide disagreement over the treatment that free persons may receive regarding the five dimensions—for instance, whether free persons should be punished. But these disagreements are based on considerations that go beyond the question of whether persons are free, because they involve substantive differences in psychological or moral theory.

In sum, the prospect that persons may satisfy the ascription of the core of moral properties (1–5) keeps incompatibilists and compatibilists at their tasks. The incompatibilists think that determinism undermines them all, and the libertarians seek to produce a variety of free will that can underwrite the whole group. Genuine compatibilists believe that we can underwrite the entire conjunction even if all choices are determined. (In my terminology, philosophers who call themselves *compatibilists* but do not try to support the existence of moral properties [1–5] are not defenders of free will.) So if we can show that determinism facilitates only some of the conjuncts and disables others, and that indeterminism facilitates only some of the conjuncts while disabling others, then whether determinism is true or not, free will cannot underwrite the conjunction. Since free will exists only if it can, free will cannot exist, whether our choices are determined or not.

5. Reasons to Reject Cockburn's Move

My rebuttal to the *bald* example lends itself to addressing the variant of the fragmentation-is-no-problem objection provided by David Cockburn. Cockburn warns us against assuming that *free will* and *moral responsibility* are *metaphysical* notions that require some feature of the world to justify their application (1992, 386–87). But this is exactly what we must assume, *if* we view the free will problem from either variety of Philosophy as Worldview Construction, that is, Philosophy as Continuous with Science or Philosophy as Non-Continuous with Science. On this view, in asking whether there can be free will, we are asking whether there can be a non-linguistic class of choices that are themselves free and that a philosophical account of free will might describe.

Those who hold Philosophy as Continuous with Science do not ask whether there is any moral benefit to keeping the vocabulary of free will and moral responsibility. Perhaps the vocabulary has a beneficial overall effect, but perhaps, as many have suggested, the vocabulary is morally oppressive. For me, the question of the effects of the vocabulary of freedom is not a *philosophical* question at all, but one for social scientists. The most that philosophers can do is speculate about whether we are better off with or without the vocabulary of free will, and I do not believe that armchair ruminations about questions in social science are worth very much. But whether the vocabulary of freedom is valuable or harmful, this is not a relevant consideration according to Philosophy as Continuous with Science. Similarly, on this metaphilosophy we give no special weight to the fact that free will supports our commonsense way of looking at ourselves.

In reading Cockburn's review of my 1991 book, my first thought was that by conceding that there is no answer to the dispute between the incompatibilists and compatibilists, Cockburn had conceded my thesis that there is no such non-linguistic *thing* as free will. But Cockburn doubts that the fragmentation of free choice shows that free will cannot exist. Suppose that I were to respond that what I *mean* when I say that free will cannot exist is simply that which Cockburn has already conceded: that it is impossible for there to be a unified class of choices that underwrites the five moral properties cited in the previous section, whether determinism is true or not. After all, I never denied that there could exist some types of free will that could underwrite *some* of the properties that we prephilosophically believe free persons to enjoy. The non-reality of free will just means that there is no single class of choices that might underwrite the whole package of deserved reactive attitudes, deserved moral praise and censure, deserved punishment and reward, special 'free agent dignity,' and autonomy.

Cockburn generously offers (in correspondence) a response to this challenge: "Even if there is no such thing as 'justifying our notion of freedom by appeal to ontology' there might (i) be such a thing as some form of ethical justification of it, (ii) whether or not there is that, it might be that if you are going to apply the [free will] notion there are, in many cases, straightforward objective tests for its application."

I am delighted with this response, because, expressed in my terms, Cockburn has reminded us that there are metaphilosophies that deny the need for ontological justifications for solutions to philosophical problems. This, of course, is one of the main theses of this book. Cockburn's reply will be available to those who hold the appropriate metaphilosophies, but the two avenues that Cockburn suggests cannot be used by the advocate of Philosophy as Continuous with Science.

Concerning point (i), according to Philosophy as Continuous with Science, the claim that there may be *moral* justifications for including free will and the various moral properties in our worldview is simply irrelevant. On this metaphilosophy, we may countenance a moral argument to the conclusion that we should *pretend* to believe in an implausible entity or *wish* that an implausible entity exists, but this would not count as grounds for actually *including* that entity in our worldview. (Compare this with the 'moral argument' for the existence of God: We could agree with Kant that it would be morally desirable to believe in the existence of God and deny that this lends any support to including God in our worldview.) On Philosophy as Non-Continuous with Science, things are a little murkier. Theorists who hold that metaphilosophy might be tempted to give some extra weight to including entities in our worldview if those entities seem morally valuable. Concerning (ii), the fact that we can continue to wield the vocabulary of freedom without ontological or moral justifications seems a strange reason to believe in free will according to either advocate of Philosophy as Worldview Construction. Why should the fact that we can talk in certain ways support any candidate's admittance into our worldview?

Cockburn's points are more persuasive when conjoined to supporting metaphilosophies. Point (i) expresses Philosophy as Praxis. On that metaphilosophy, moral justifications are given the sort of priority Cockburn suggests they may be given: They override the lack of ontological justifications. So Praxis makes Cockburn's first point look more persuasive. Point (ii) expresses Philosophy as Underpinnings for Common Sense. On this metaphilosophy, everyday discourse provides its own rationale for asserting that things exist, apart from those rationales given by the ontologists and moralists. In this instance, Underpinnings is helped out by the instrumentalist interpretation of theories from chapter 3: We do not need an ontological proof of freedom before we can say that freedom is real.

I confess that I am not altogether certain how persuasive Cockburn's reply to the fragmentation problem is even if we accept Philosophy as Praxis or Philosophy as Underpinnings for Common Sense. Regarding the latter, if I am right in my claim that common sense sees free persons as loci for the five moral properties in question, then Cockburn's admission that persons cannot enjoy the whole package would appear to undermine rather than underpin common sense. At the very least, this would mark a very *revisionistic* bit of underpinning. Regarding the motivation of justifying moral notions in Philosophy as Praxis, I think that the results also may be unpromising for the defenders of free will. At the level of moral practice, we may need to assume that free will justifies a coherent, unified picture of free and responsible persons. Perhaps some looseness is possible, but I doubt that there can be as much looseness as is implied by the admission that there is no correct answer to the dispute between the incompatibilists and the compatibilists. I suspect that the practice of viewing persons as responsible may require more unity than that.

6. Mele's Objection

In discussing *The Non-Reality of Free Will* in his *Autonomous Agents*, Alfred Mele argues that even if there were no truth to whether the incompatibilists or compatibilists are correct, this would not prove that free will cannot exist:

> Consider an analogy. There is an ongoing dispute about what actions are and about how 'action' is to be analyzed. The range of acceptable options has been narrowed down (in my opinion) to a few; but (again, in my opinion) no one has offered conclusive grounds for accepting one of the options in preference to the others. Suppose that "there is no way to adjudicate the dispute about who is right" and that there is no fact of the matter about whether any of the live options is (exclusively) the best option. Would it follow—in light of the fact that having performed an intentional action requires having performed an action—that there is no such thing as intentional action, that no one ever acts intentionally?
>
> Of course not. We can have excellent evidence that people sometimes act intentionally, even if . . . 'action' may be understood in way *x* or in way *y*, . . . and "there is no way to adjudicate the dispute about who is right" about 'action.' . . . Similarly, making the parallel supposition about free will and 'could have chosen otherwise' does not itself commit one to holding that no one has free will. Perhaps we can have free will even if there is no fact of the matter about whether 'could have chosen otherwise' is to be understood along compatibilist or libertarian lines. (1995, chapter 13)

Before replying to this objection, let me distinguish my argument from another that is similar to it, although Mele does not confuse the two. I do not argue that because we do not *know* whether incompatibilism or compatibilism gives the correct account of free will, free will cannot exist. It is not that I think that this would be a *terrible* argument. If we view philosophers' collective indecision over the debate between the incompatibilists and the compatibilists as data in need of an explanation, the explanation that there *is* no such thing as free will is probably as good as any. But the free will realist can reply that although one side is right, it is just very difficult to know which side it is. So using philosophers' indecision over this issue would not provide a decisive argument for nonrealism. This is not my argument. My argument is that because neither incompatibilism nor compatibilism *is* correct, this provides strong, though not logically conclusive, reason to think that free will does not exist. This is my fragmentation argument.

Here is my reply to Mele's analogy. I begin with the premise that Mele grants for the sake of criticizing my argument: that there *is* no truth to the matter about whether the compatibilists or incompatibilists are right about what free choice requires. Recall from chapter 6 the four theses (IN), (IP), (CN), and (CP) and the four theories predicated upon the assumption that the four theses take truth-values. (IN) maintains that determined choices cannot be free, (IP) maintains that undetermined choices can be free, (CN) says that undetermined choices cannot be free, and (CP) says that determined choices can be free. If we accept (IN) and (IP) we are Classical Incompatibilists; (CN) and (CP) yield Classical Compatibilism; (IP) and (CP) yield the Free-Will-Either-Way Theory; and (IN) and (CN) yield the No-Free-Will-Either-Way Theory.

To grant—even for the sake of argument—my claim that there is no correct answer to the debate between the incompatibilists and compatibilists would be to eliminate Classical Incompatibilism and Classical Compatibilism. For if either of the classical theories is correct, then the other classical theory is incorrect, and, thus, there *is* a definite answer to the debate between the incompatibilists and the compatibilists. This leaves three possibilities: the No-Free-Will-Either-Way Theory, the Free-Will-Either-Way Theory, and my subjectivist view that none of the constituent statements (IN), (IP), (CN), or (CP) can be objectively true.

If we accept the No-Free-Will-Either-Way Theory, then we accept a variety of free will non-realism. Admittedly, this is not the subjectivist version of non-realism that I endorse, but it is nonetheless a view that denies that anyone enjoys free will. So it looks as if the only way that Mele's objection can help the free will realist is by presupposing that the Free-Will-Either-Way Theory is correct. For all I know, some analogue to this theory is an acceptable account of *action*. But the Free-Will-Either-Way Theory faces serious difficulties.

The Free-Will-Either-Way Theory seems to me the least attractive of the four theories predicated on the four free will theses. As noted in chapter 6, this theory endorses the weakest theses of the compatibilists and incompatibilists, (IP) and (CP), while rejecting their strongest theses, (IN) and (CN). By maintaining that both determinism and indeterminism pose no problem for freedom, the Free-Will-Either-Way Theory faces a withering crossfire of objections from both the incompatibilists and the compatibilists. We reasonably might face such an attack if we had antecedent reasons for supposing that free will exists. But we do not, unlike the case where we are convinced that intentional action exists regardless of what we think about the theoretical analysis of action.

This suggests that Mele's example, though effective as a logical analogy to show that my fragmentation premise does not *entail* subjectivism, does not damage my fragmentation argument when it is understood non-deductively. Mele's analogy is not all that analogous, and this means that the supporter of the fragmentation-is-no-problem response is unlikely to find in it the resources to undermine my overall strategy. On Mele's analogy, although theorists disagree over the best technical account of *action*, their disagreements do not show the existence of either actions or intentional actions to be doubtful. It is clear why. There are overwhelming reasons for believing in actions and intentional actions that do not depend on anyone's having a finished account of *action*. First, we can satisfy ourselves that actions and intentional actions exist in the first person by noticing our ability to affect the world. Second, we can justify the existence of intentional actions and actions per se because, tautologically, the postulation of intentional actions provides the best theoretical explanation of human behavior. The existence of intentional actions and actions, thus, is not jeopardized by theoretical disagreements about *action*.

On the other hand, talk about the freeness of choices is icing on the behavioral cake, handy in moralizing (and in trying to justify retribution) but not needed for the explanation of human and animal behavior. Controversy arises over the existence of freeness, not over the existence of choices. The existence of choices can be justified by the same sort of evidence that justifies the existence of action. The freeness of choices, on the other hand, cannot be justified in either of these ways but stands in need of a theoretical account. Difficulties in giving a theoretical account weighs much more heavily against free choices than against actions.

7. Conclusion

The fragmentation in our thinking about free will suggests that there is no objective characteristic of actions that underwrites the ascription of the family of moral notions centered around moral responsibility. The fragmentation objection is persuasive if we adopt Philosophy as Continuous with Science and the intermediate philosophical principles that go along with it. The two objections examined in this chapter—that fragmentation does not occur and that even if it does it would not provide a problem for the existence of free will—are unpersuasive when taken by themselves. These criticisms become more powerful if we add Praxis or

Underpinnings metaphilosophies. It is conceivable that these criticisms might appear *very* persuasive on these alternative metaphilosophies, but I shall not examine that possibility. In the next two chapters I continue the role of partisan on behalf of Philosophy as Continuous with Science by showing how the moral character of *free will* supports subjectivism for those who accept the metaphilosophy I do.

8

Free Will Is a Moral Concept

In this chapter I argue that when we add *free* to the psychological words *choice* and *will*, the result is a moral concept. If *free choice* is moral and if there are no objective moral truths, then there are no objective truths about free will. I do not argue for the moral non-realist premise, although I have done so (Double, 1991B, chapter 7) and others have given what I think are highly persuasive arguments (Hume; Williams, 1973 and 1981; Mackie, 1977; Harman, 1977; Blackburn, 1984). Within the framework of this book I do not need to argue for moral non-realism, because part II presupposes Philosophy as Continuous with Science and the intermediate principles that go along with it. Given those premises, it will be enough for my purposes if I can show that *free choice* is moral. In chapter 9 I reinforce the argument of this chapter and go a step further. There I argue that if we accept the Humean principle that moral conclusions cannot be derived from non-moral premises, we can show both that *free choice* is a moral notion *and* that ascriptions of free choice cannot be true.

Strictly speaking, the premise that *free choice* is a moral term is stronger than I need for the subjectivist argument in this book. If I establish merely that philosophers view free choice as a moral good, then according to moral non-realism it will follow that there can be no free choices. I wish to argue for the semantic claim, however, because: (1) I believe that it is true and not widely recognized, and (2) all the arguments that I present to support my view that *free choice* is a moral concept will more clearly support, *en passant*, the notion that philosophers treat free choice as a moral good.

In section 1, I say what I mean by calling a term *moral*. In section 2, I give a preliminary reason for thinking that *free choice* is moral. In section 3, I offer an analogy between *goodness* and *freeness* based on G. E. Moore's open-question argument to show that *free choice* is moral. In section 4, I show how judgments about free will satisfy Gilbert Harman's (1977) analysis of the way in which moral 'observations' are unlike scientific observations. This suggests that the judgments of the incompatibilists and compatibilists are moral also. In section 5, I examine the disagreement between the incompatibilists and compatibilists over whether free will requires ultimate responsibility or ultimacy, "the condition that an agent's . . . decision or choice should not be caused by factors for which he is not responsible" (Klein, 1990, 49). Noting some of the rhetorical devices that appear in this discussion, I develop an argument to show that the question of whether free will requires ultimacy (which appears to be a conceptual dispute over the correct definition of *freedom*) depends on whether ultimacy is desirable. In Section 6, I provide a similar argument, this time focusing on the attitudinal nature of the disagreement over whether compatibilists are 'magnanimous' to hold that determined persons can be free.

1. What Does It Mean to Call *Free Choice* a Moral Term?

Because I accept the fact/value distinction and the doctrine of the non-definability of moral terms by non-moral terms, I find saying exactly what I mean by *moral* somewhat tricky. I could provide some idea of what I mean by offering an enumeration of terms that are generally recognized as moral (*good, evil, right*, etc.), but this would not help my aim of showing that a term that is not widely regarded as moral really is moral. Nor would a strict account that held that a moral term is one whose analysis explicitly requires the mention of one of the generally recognized moral terms. (I owe this suggestion to Tomis Kapitan.) A more illuminating account provided by John Searle shows what makes moral terms moral.

Extrapolating from Searle's speech-act analysis, *free* in *free choice* might be moral even if we do not *have* to define it in terms of generally recognized moral terms. According to Searle's analysis, the definitive characteristic of evaluative terms generally is that we cannot treat the appropriateness of their application as one matter and their illocutionary or 'emotive' force as another. For evaluative terms, once we have decided that S is a p, we have already decided that S's being a p is a good or bad thing, and *saying* that S is or is not p is to evaluate S (Searle, 1969, chapter 6). Applying Searle's account, I believe that *calling* choices *free* expresses a positive rating of those choices on a moral scale.

The weaker claim that free choice is treated as a moral good is easier to establish. Philosophers believe that it is better morally to make free than unfree choices. This is not to say that we believe that choosing freely always makes us better off than choosing unfreely. We can make sense out of the idea that sometimes an escape from freedom is desirable. Nonetheless, philosophers believe that a world of free agents is morally preferable to a world of unfree agents.

Consider the libertarian's free will defense in the problem of evil. First, the value of our having libertarian undetermined free choices is supposed to outweigh the moral badness of the evil those choices sometimes produce. It seems plausible to impute to libertarians the belief that only moral goodness morally outweighs moral evil. Second, the freeness of our choices is supposed to warrant God's retribution, performing the remarkable feat of turning an otherwise morally bad thing (intentionally inflicted suffering) into a moral good (just deserts). Here, too, it seems that only a moral good could do the trick. Now, if I can show that we not only endorse free choices (i.e., view free choices as a moral good) but also, in our very act of calling choices *free*, offer a positive evaluation, I will have supported the semantic thesis of this chapter.

2. A Preliminary Reason for Thinking That *Free Choice* Is Moral

A preliminary reason to think that *free choice* is moral is the role that ascriptions of free choice play in justifying ascriptions of moral responsibility. First, although some philosophers argue that we can be morally responsible for omissions (where we did not exercise free will), a standard defeating objection to ascriptions of moral responsibility is that we chose *un*freely. So the ascription of free choice looks to be a necessary condition for the application of a moral concept, at least as a reply to the excuse that we were unfree. Second, *free choice* plays a role in positively justifying ascriptions of moral responsibility. In the first chapter, I defined *free choices* as choices that are good enough to make us morally responsible for the actions they produce unless some excusing condition obtains. Some free will theorists claim not to be very interested in moral responsibility (Kevin Magill in correspondence), and they are entitled to care about whatever they want. There is, of course, a familiar compatibilist move that reminds us that determinism is compatible with many varieties of free action that have little to do with moral responsibility, a move that incompatibilists correctly regard as an evasion of their concern. It would smack of sour grapes for compatibilists to disparage the attempt to vindicate moral responsibility on coming to the conclusion that they cannot succeed.

The connection between freedom and responsibility that most free will theorists care about becomes more clear if we focus on the role that the ascription of free choice plays in justifying our treatment of persons. Consider these premises.

(A) *Ascriptions of free choice are used to justify the negative treatment of persons.* (This includes the expression of negative reactive attitudes, blame, and punishment.) (A) is a sociological generalization that we can justify in armchair fashion. It does not merely claim that freedom is treated as a necessary condition for justifying the negative treatment of persons. (A) asserts that "S is free" is used to play a positive role in justifying the treatment of S, and not just the negative role of foreclosing the objection that we cannot treat S badly because S is unfree. Used positively, the claim that S is free is used to argue that we are morally right to express reactive attitudes or blame or punish S *because* S is free. It is the positive use of ascriptions to justify blame that most clearly support the thesis that *free* is moral.

(B) *Only the ascription of a moral property justifies the negative treatment of persons.* This is a moral claim. We can understand it as an expression of a deontological principle: We may not treat persons negatively unless they have made themselves appropriate candidates for such treatment because they have acted immorally. Consequentialists also would accept this principle, because they believe that consequential properties are moral properties. So if consequences justify the negative treatment of persons and consequences are moral, then moral properties justify the negative treatment of persons.

I believe that these premises independently support, though do not entail, three conclusions. The most obvious seems to be (C1): *If ascriptions of free choice are to succeed in justifying the negative treatment of persons, then those ascriptions must be moral.* The two premises also yield (C2): *Ascriptions-of-free-choice are ascriptions-of-moral-properties.* (The hyphenation is used to emphasize that these ascriptions do imply the reality of that which is 'ascribed.') Finally, the two premises support the conclusion (C3): *'Free choice' (due to its use) is a moral notion.* This final conclusion relies on the doctrine of meaning as use.

One could reject the above argument by saying that (B), as a moral premise, cannot serve in my argument because moral claims are neither true nor false. Strictly speaking, this application of moral non-realism would disable my preliminary argument that *free choice* is a moral notion. Dialectically, though, this would be a poor move by the defender of the objectivity of free will, because: (1) I have several other arguments to show that *free choice* is moral, and (2) accepting moral non-realism, in the long run, will hurt the defense of free will realism more than accepting my argument that *free choice* is moral.

3. The Open-Question Argument:
Goodness and *Freeness*

I want to press the role that ascriptions of free choice play by developing an analogy between using *free choice* to justify blame and G. E. Moore's (1968) open-question argument. Moore construes his naturalistic opponents as analytically defining *moral goodness* with attempts like "what produces pleasure" or "what contributes to the evolution of the species." Moore objects that it is an open question to ask whether that which produces pleasure is good or whether that which contributes to evolution is good. On the assumption that analytic definitions would not leave questions like this open, it follows that the naturalistic proposals cannot be analytic.

Suppose we try to justify blaming Mr. M by claiming that M meets some factual conditions (satisfies a naturalistic account) of free choice, but we resist acknowledging *free choice* to be a moral notion. If we are libertarians we might say, "You were the ultimate, undetermined originator of your choice." The trouble with this attempt at justification is that M can reply in the Hobart-Schlick-Ayer tradition that his choice was not under his rational control, hence, he was not free, hence, he is blameless. If we are compatibilists we might say that M's determined choice satisfies, for example, Harry Frankfurt's hierarchical account of free choice. But then M can use incompatibilist intuitions to excuse himself: "I am determined, hence unfree, hence blameless." If we do not take a stand on whether M's choice was determined or undetermined, then M is free to claim either that his choice was undetermined, hence unfree, *or* that it was determined, hence unfree.

The only way to prevent M from making one of these moves is to *stipulate* that M chose A freely in the moral-responsibility-justifying sense I am using in this book. Such a stipulation thwarts M's complaint whether based on the grounds that he was determined, that he was undetermined, or even that free choice is not possible whether our choices are determined or not. *Saying* that a blamee chose from free will (i.e., using the term *free will*) performs a similar role in justifying punishment that *saying* something is morally good (i.e., using the term *morally good*) does in justifying the claim that something is good. We do not rebut Moore's semantic challenge by referring to goodness using naturalistic terms (even if goodness *is* a naturalistic property). We do not justify blame until we cite free choice using the term *free choice* (even if free choice *is* what the libertarians or compatibilists say it is). This shows that the assertion that one chooses freely performs an analogous semantic role to saying something is good. In the performance of each speech act we close the question.

We have not justified blame so long as our justifications would be acceptable only by particular constituencies such as the incompatibilists or compatibilists. We cannot succeed in justifying blame if the conception of *free choice* that we use is 'naturalistically' explicated in terms of the non-moral metaphysical definitions of the compatibilists or incompatibilists. Thus, we have to express something more than a descriptive libertarian or compatibilist account of *free choice*. This strongly suggests that only the application of *free choice* with its full moral force will provide a justification of blame that commands enough illocutionary force to do the job.

Let me summarize my argument as a *reductio*:

(a) Suppose that *free choice* is not a moral concept that is indefinable in terms of non-moral metaphysical concepts.
(b) Then, *free choice* can be defined by such concepts. (From [a])
(c) If (b), then citing some correct set of non-moral metaphysical concepts will play the role in justifying blame that citing free will does. (Conceptual role semantics)
(d) There is good reason to think that there is no set of non-moral metaphysical conditions that will play this role. (Libertarian and compatibilist accounts of free choice fail, as noted)

(e) Therefore, there is good reason to think that *free choice* is a moral concept.

4. The Analogy with Moral Facts:
Freeness Facts Have No Explanatory Power

Gilbert Harman (1977) invokes a powerful weapon against moral realism by arguing for the explanatory uselessness of postulating moral facts. Although I believe that Harman's argument is as close to a refutation of moral realism as we are likely to get, here I use Harman's reasoning to support only the thesis that *free will* is a moral concept. This is the argument I propose: (i) Harman's argument demonstrates what feature makes 'moral facts' moral. (This is a datum that no one denies.) (ii) Freeness facts, if they were to exist, would possess the same feature that makes moral facts moral. (iii) So, by analogy, if freeness facts exist, they are moral.

Harman emphasizes the different role that moral and scientific principles play in explaining observations:

> Observational evidence plays a part in science it does not appear to play in ethics, because scientific principles can be justified ultimately by their role in explaining observations . . . by their explanatory role. Apparently, moral principles cannot be justified in the same way. It appears . . . that there can be no explanatory chain between moral principles and particular observings in the way that there can be such a chain between scientific principles and particular observings. Conceived as an explanatory theory, morality, unlike science, seems to be cut off from observation. (1977, 9)

Harman illustrates the difference this way:

> Consider a physicist making an observation to test a scientific theory. Seeing a vapor trail in a cloud chamber, he thinks, "There goes a proton." . . . He can count his making the observation as confirming evidence for his theory only to the extent that it is reasonable to explain his making the observation by assuming that, not only is he in a certain psychological "set," given the theory he accepts and his beliefs about the experimental apparatus, but furthermore, there really was a proton going through the cloud chamber, causing the vapor trail, which he saw as a proton. . . . But, if his having made that observation could have been equally well explained by his psychological set alone, without the need for any assumption about a proton,

the observation would not have been evidence for the existence of that proton and therefore would not have been evidence for the theory. . . .

    Compare this case with one in which you make a moral judgment immediately and without conscious reasoning, say, that the children are wrong to set the cat on fire. . . . [A]n assumption about moral facts would seem to be totally irrelevant to the explanation of your making the judgment you make. It would seem that all we need assume is that you have certain more or less well articulated moral principles that are reflected in the judgments you make, based on your moral sensibility. It seems to be completely irrelevant to our explanation whether your intuitive immediate judgment is true or false. (1977, 6–7)

From the standpoint of explanation, freeness facts are like moral facts. As a non-behaviorist, I believe that the postulation of persons' and animals' *choices* can be justified as a better explanation for observed behavior than an ontological (rather than methodological) behaviorism that denies the existence of choices. Philosophically, we must leave room for an intervening variable that underlies the ability of persons and animals to act in different ways, even if the methodological behaviorists are right in thinking that intervening psychological variables are not needed to predict behavior. Otherwise, we could not make sense of the fact that positive reinforcement increases frequency of response: for example, the rat *chooses* to take the left path through the maze because it has received sugar-water in the past by going left. If the rat does not choose to go left, then the fact that it goes left is mysteriously connected with its reinforcement history. (If I am wrong about this and there are no choices, then, *ipso facto*, there are no *free* choices, and this provides a cheap route to the non-reality of free choices.)

But whether the rat that was positively reinforced to run left chooses to go left *freely* has no use in explaining any observation. *Free* in this case is an honorific term that has no explanatory role. This point is even more clear if we ask whether the rat's choice is free when the rat is placed in the maze for the first time without prior reinforcement and we hypothesize that the rat chooses under the condition of universal determinism. The purported freeness fact that is disputed by the incompatibilists and the compatibilists concerning determinism per se does not help explain: (i) anything about the rat's behavior, nor (ii) anything about our assessments of the rat's freedom. Our application of the term *free* can be explained entirely by reference to our theoretical beliefs about free will and determinism. Changing *moral* to *freeness* in the penultimate line in the passage from Harman above, we could say, "It would seem that all we need assume is that you have certain more or less well articulated freeness principles that are reflected in the judgments you make, based on your freeness sensibility."

'Moral facts' are moral because they express feelings and attitudes that persons have for or against things. Thus, to explain why someone expressed a 'moral fact,' we need only to cite what Harman calls the *psychological set* of the expressor. There is no *need* to consult the world outside the evaluator. This is exactly the case with the 'freeness facts' of the free will realist. It may be imaginable that standing behind our freeness attitudes, there could be an objective, non-attitudinal freeness fact (just as objective moral truth may be imaginable). There seems to be no explanatory reason to postulate it, however. But whether I am right about that or not, the analogy between freeness facts and moral facts strongly supports the view that *free will* is moral.

5. The Goodness of Ultimacy

In some very important books and articles, Robert Kane (1985, 1988, 1989, 1990, 1996) has argued that our being ultimately responsible for our actions is crucial to libertarian ideas about free will. For Kane, a person is the ultimate cause of a choice only if "no set of conditions not including the choice itself is sufficient for either its occurrence or its rationality" (1990, 7). Kane believes that this aspect of ultimacy commits libertarians to indeterminism, not because libertarians like indeterminism per se but because they realize that determinism would violate ultimacy. Kane cites Aristotle's claim in the *Nicomachean Ethics* (Book III, Ch. 5) that in order for a man to be responsible for acts issuing from his character, he must be responsible for his character having become the way it is (1996, chapter 3). According to Kane, if determinism were true, then our choices could be traced back to the antecedent causal nature of the world, with causal responsibility being traced before us to nature or God.

Martha Klein explains the incompatibilist's penchant for ultimacy this way:

> [The incompatibilist's] conviction, that one of the things that disqualifies an agent from blameworthiness is his not having been responsible for the causes of his decisions or choices, commits him to the belief that it is a condition of agent accountability that agents should be ultimately responsible for their morally relevant decisions or choices—'ultimately' in the

sense that nothing for which they are not responsible should be the source of their decisions or choices. (1990, 51)

Ultimacy is examined under the banner of *true responsibility* (G. Strawson, 1986, chapter 2), *autonomy* (Wolf, 1990, chapter 2), and *sole authorship* (Nathan, 1992, 32–37).

It is possible to *state* the need for ultimacy dispassionately, but the rhetoric heats up when philosophers try to *argue* for and against it. Much of what is presented by the libertarians and compatabilists on whether freedom requires ultimacy (and indeterminism) can be subsumed under two headings, which I call an *appeal to glory* and an *appeal to fear*.

For libertarians, the appeal to glory has several threads. The inspirational thought that we are 'above' nature—that humans really are more noble than the rest of 'mere' nature—is an important theme for Descartes, Kant, and many other theological and quasi-theological thinkers. This glorification theme has appeal even to the atheist Sartre (1956), who locates freedom within our distinctive *pour soi* and declares that we are "condemned" to be free. Kane finds such non-physicalist positions ontologically extravagant, but he still appeals to an executive metaphor to support the demand for ultimacy: Only ultimacy establishes that "the buck stops here" with respect to our choices (1989, 225).

The idea that undetermined choices make us *unique* also plays a part in glorifying ultimacy. Kane believes that only libertarian free will enables persons to be unique in a way that is a precondition for several valuable traits, including, among others: being appropriately subject to desert for our accomplishments, ascriptions of moral responsibility, and reactive attitudes, love, and friendship; being worthy of dignity, love, and friendship; and displaying genuine creativity and autonomy (1994A, 83; 1996, chapter 6). According to Richard Rorty, the poet Philip Larkin believes that unless he makes a unique contribution to culture, he has made none and he has been no one. Rorty interprets Larkin's worry this way:

What he fears will be extinguished is his idiosyncratic lading-list, his individual sense of what is possible and important. That is what made his I different from all other I's. To lose that difference is . . . what any poet— any maker, anyone who hopes to create something new—fears. . . . But this does not mean simply that one fears that one's works will be lost or ignored. For that fear blends into the fear that, even if they are preserved and noticed, nobody will find anything distinctive in them. The words . . . marshalled to one's command may seem merely stock items, rearranged in routine ways. One will not have impressed one's mark on the language, but, rather, will have spent one's life shoving about already coined pieces. *So one will not really have had an I at all. One's creations, and one's self, will just be better or worse instances of familiar types.* (1989, 23–24, my italics)

Evidently the libertarian Kane is not so far removed from the poet Larkin (or Rorty's Larkin) on the importance of being unique.

The appeal to fear takes several forms for the libertarians. Libertarians sometimes portray non-ultimacy (i.e., determinism) as fatalism, worrying us with the thought that without ultimacy we lack efficacy over our choices and our lives. A similar persuasive device is the fear of cosmic manipulators who are super-added to the determined etiology of our choices—whether the traditional omniscient, omnipotent Christian God or analytic philosophy's 'bug bears' (Dennett's 1984 word) such as remote controllers from Mars. Advocates of ultimacy sometimes raise the specter of mechanism—the fear that without ultimacy we would no longer be rational agents, but instead big stupid clocks who do not track truth on the basis of reasons but believe only what we are caused to believe (Popper, 1965; Lucas, 1993, 29–32). Less drastically, Kane thinks that entertaining the possibility of determinism "poses a . . . threat to the human self image and a corresponding crisis in human thinking," because determinism would mean that "we are not really independent sources of motion in the world at all, but products of the world" (1996, chapter 6). Finally, William James assails determinism for its commitment to the *iron block universe* that

professes that those parts of the universe already laid down appoint and decree what other parts shall be. The future has no ambiguous possibilities hidden in its womb; the part we call the present is compatible with only one totality. Any future complement than the one fixed from eternity is impossible. The whole is in each and every part, and welds it with the rest into an absolute unity, an iron block, in which there can be no equivocation or shadow of turning. (1962, 150)

Compatibilists often represent determinism in a laudatory light: Deterministic nature is *good*. We should live in harmony with nature. Deterministic nature is really 'God,' according to Spinoza. Nature and we are one, as modes of God, if only we could come to realize it. According to Ted Honderich, "there has been a long history of thought and feeling which has to do in a certain way with our relation to nature. In part, this has involved the recommendation that we somehow get into connection with it, somehow identify or associate ourselves with it, or at least be guided by it. The idea is that there is a great reward in this" (1993, 113). While glorifying nature, compatibilists also have stressed the fear of irrationality. Frankfurt (1971, 77) and Dennett (1984, 172) challenge us to say what *more* we could want for free beings than that they make reflective, self-conscious choices. Other compatibilists have claimed that ultimacy necessarily brings with it choices that are uncaused, hence not caused by our psychological states, hence sporadic, random, crazy, and so on (Hobart, 1934; Ayer, 1954).

Even the libertarians and compatibilists who make these rhetorical moves must admit that these lines of persuasion do not look quite like the arguments used in linguistic analysis. It is not that the examples are more bizarre than the 'Gettier-examples' used in the debate over the definition of propositional knowledge or the fission/fusion examples used in discussions of personal identity. The difference is that the free will discussions speak to an issue beyond mere conceptual analysis: the *goodness* or *desirability* of ultimacy as well as its *relevance* to free will. The rhetorical maneuvers are designed to stir emotion and move attitudes, to shock and to inspire. These typically are the tools of value theory, and they show that free will is being treated as a moral good. This observation suggests a further argument that *free will* is a moral term.

I begin the argument by contrasting two questions: (i) *Is ultimacy a necessary condition of free choices?* (ii) *Is ultimacy a desirable characteristic of human choices?* Question (i) is a conceptual one about a metaphysical topic. If it could be addressed without broaching the issue of how valuable we think ultimacy is, then it would seem clearly nonevaluative. Question (ii) belongs to value theory, because it asks whether a characteristic is intrinsically worth having: Is it better morally for persons to be the ultimate causes of their choices or not?

Consider the concept *cat*. Suppose we wish to decide whether a necessary condition of being a cat is being an evolved animal as opposed to being, for example, a cleverly disguised artifact put on Earth by Martian remote controllers (Putnam, 1962, 660). Here we are not concerned with the question of whether it is 'good' to be an animal with the normal etiology as opposed to being an artifact. The question, instead, is conceptual: Does the concept *cat* guarantee that real cats are not artifacts? This is a paradigm of a conceptual issue involving a non-evaluative concept.

Consider next the concept *morally perfect being*. Suppose we were to ask whether valuing retribution more than compassion is consistent with being a morally perfect being. In this case, the question (iii) *"Is the characteristic of valuing retribution more than compassion a condition that debars one from being a morally perfect being?"* logically presupposes an answer to the question to (iv) *"Is the characteristic of valuing retribution more than compassion a good characteristic per se?"* Logically, there is no answer to (iii) unless there is an answer to (iv), because the concept *morally perfect being* excludes the possibility that a being that correctly answers to that concept could possess morally defective characteristics. This illustrates what is obvious, namely, that *morally perfect being* is a moral concept.

The debate over the goodness of ultimacy illustrates that *free choice* is like *morally perfect being* and not like *cat*. If the debate over including ultimacy in the analysis of *free will* could be limited to the discussion of (i), then that debate would clearly concern the analysis of a non-evaluative metaphysical concept. Libertarians and compatibilists might offer opinions concerning (ii), but that would be an analytically separable enterprise. But, in fact, we are unable to analyze the concept *free* and decide whether free persons must be the ultimate causes of their choices without first deciding whether to endorse our being the ultimate causes of our choices. Once the issue of the goodness of ultimacy arises, an explanation for the above fact is needed. That *free will* is a moral term explains the debate. I admit that it is still possible that *free will* is a non-moral concept, and that philosophers are simply treating free will as a moral good. But given the role that citing ultimacy plays in the free will debate, and given the premise of conceptual role semantics used in the previous sections of this chapter, the conceptual claim seems warranted.

6. The Dispute over Magnanimity

Compatibilists have another powerful rhetorical line: "We compatibilists are *magnanimous* in the face of determinism; we accept nature, recognize that we are part of it, and are at peace with it and ourselves. You libertarians—who want to carve out a special niche in the cosmos for free agents, however incomprehensible it might be—are insufficiently magnanimous. You are vain, antagonistic toward the cosmos, and too quick to fly to extravagances to aggrandize yourselves. You should accept your freedom as it is and try to enhance it as you can, rather than engage in fanciful speculations that evince your psychological weaknesses.

"Consider the mean-spiritedness of your position. You crave indeterminism ('ultimacy' is just a way to put a favorable gloss on indeterminism) because it would foil any covert non-constraining controller (Kane's 1985 word), including God, from being able to completely dictate our choices. You seek indeterminism in your choices because you think that it is not enough that *your* decisions produce your actions. You demand further that there be no causal history through which your decisions can be traced (McCall, 1984, 333), even though you want your decisions to cause your behavior and realize that determinism is not fatalism.

"This is a petty attitude, because it emphasizes an entirely *negative* condition. Indeterminacy does not empower us relative to how we would be in a determined cosmos. Indeterminism does not make our choices smarter, more under our control, or better in any positive way. If anything, indeterminism would make our choices less under our rational control. The only advantage to indeterminism is that it might weaken the power of a controller, and if there is no such controller, then indeterminism does not even yield this benefit. So indeterminism does not help us, it probably hurts us, and its only selling point is that it might foil the complete control of a controller, if one existed. (Even this is not much, because such a controller could set up undesirable alternatives between which we would make indeterministic choices that would leave us woefully unfree under the controller's disjunctive control [Double, 1991B, 214–15].) If we were to evaluate the libertarian proposal as we do public policy, we could not endorse it. It represents a state of affairs that benefits no one, where everyone is likely to be made worse off, and is justified by the hope of making a (probably) mythical entity worse off. This is a low-minded, carping attitude that is unworthy of philosophers."

Libertarians can respond to this rhetoric with their own views about the compatibilist magnanimity in the face of determinism: "Such 'high-mindedness' is really self-deception that tries to palliate a dreary possibility without bothering to explore what intellectual work can be done to avoid it. Compatibilism—because it does not require the postulation of non-physical minds, the persons of agent theory, or amplifications of quantum indeterminacies—is admittedly a cheap route to believing in free will, but it is cheap in the way that, using Bertrand Russell's expression, theft is cheaper than honest toil. If you *really* want to be magnanimous, then renounce free will and moral responsibility as the hard determinist does and face up to the unpleasant facts. Because this response to the need for ultimacy evinces self-deception, intellectual laziness, and cheap gratification, compatibilists reveal that they are short on character."

Inductively speaking, most debates over the 'right' degree of magnanimity are value debates. We might ask: How should we respond to rudeness or the careless performance of an assigned task? Are we appropriately high-minded to overlook these or should we demand better? Because the differences between the libertarians and incompatibilists are debates over how we should feel about determinism and indeterminism, this is some reason to see these debates as moral. This would place the free-will problem squarely within moral philosophy, even if we resist the conclusion that *free choice* is a moral concept.

Here is a slightly different way to look at the magnanimity dispute. Our choices can be viewed as a function of two components: our contribution and the contribution of everything else (nature, God, Martian remote controllers, etc.). If our choices are determined, then our contribution is subsumed under that of everything else. If we choose indeterministically, as the libertarians hope, then our contribution does not fall under that of everything else, and, in particular, we are outside of the deterministic web of nature. In this sense, the incompatibilist's postulation of indeterminism can be viewed as a way of *reducing* nature's role in the etiology of our choices. This would be an absolute diminution of the role of nature in our choices. But such diminution, by itself, does not produce an *enhancement* in our contribution to our choices. As far as I know, no libertarian has ever claimed that indeterminism makes our role greater in an absolute sense, but only in the comparative sense that now nature cannot be viewed as including our contribution.

Thus framed, the question is this: Should we regard the lessening of nature's role in our choices as desirable for *our* role in our choices? Comparatively speaking, what lessens nature's role in our choices enhances ours, in the way that a competitor's bad golf shot enhances your play vis-à-vis that person but does not improve your play absolutely. Absolutely speaking, the lessening of nature's role does not enhance our role, in that the diminution does not make our choices smarter, more careful, more rational, or any more under our control. To judge whether we are better off if determinism or indeterminism is the case, we have to decide whether we should adopt the comparative or absolute viewpoint. Well, to use the analogy, how *should* we feel about our well-being when that of others is diminished or enhanced in comparison to ours? This strikes me as a paradigm of an attitudinal question, not to be settled by any non-moral fact. If we believe that attitudes are incapable of being true or false, then the magnanimity issue strongly supports the subjectivism of free will.

The free will realist might reply as follows: "Even if the free will debate *is* a matter of conflicting attitudes, the *appropriateness* of our feelings about ultimacy and determinism can be rated non-attitudinally relative to the *fact* of whether determinism does or does not defeat the freeness of our choices. Facts about freeness dictate the appropriateness of our freeness attitudes." Let me respond.

Compatibilists, incompatibilists, No-Free-Will-Either-Way theorists, and Free-Will-Either-Way theorists believe that there is what I call a *freeness fact*—that is, a fact to the matter of whether determinism makes our choices unfree. Incompatibilists believe that the freeness fact is that determinism is incompatible with free will, and compatibilists believe that the freeness fact is that determinism is compatible with (and is conducive to) free will. For the four types of realists, such freeness facts exist over and beyond what I call our *freeness attitudes*, which are our positive or negative feelings about determinism. Incompatibilists express negative freeness attitudes toward the compatibility of determinism and free will, and compatibilists express pro-freeness attitudes toward the compatibility of determinism and free will.

As a subjectivist, I believe that there are only freeness attitudes and no freeness facts. If there are no freeness facts, then talk about appropriate and inappropriate freeness attitudes logically cannot be truth-valued. Such talk may be conversationally interesting or morally useful, but it cannot track truth. I believe that my view is simpler and more likely to be true than the views of any of the realists. This does not prove that there are no freeness facts, but how would one do that? This sort of consideration is sufficient, if we come to the free will problem from Philosophy as Continuous with Science. For if we rely on the intermediate principles of ontological parsimony and the fact-value distinction, then showing that the free will problem is part of moral philosophy will suffice to yield the non-realist conclusion. Once that package of metaphilosophy and intermediate principles is used to supply premises, all of the realist positions, with their commitments to freeness facts, will be untenable.

7. Conclusion

Free will is connected with moral notions such as *moral responsibility* and *desert*. Free will is treated as a moral good. Moreover, *free will* seems itself to be a moral term. Strictly speaking, the free will problem belongs to ethics, not to metaphysics. That does not settle the question of the reality of free will, because moral realism is a possible, indeed unrefutable, position. But given the package of metaphilosophy and intermediate principles that I use in part II of this book, the moral character of free will contributes mightily to rejecting its candidacy to our worldview.

If *free will* (*free choice*) is itself a moral concept, then whether we are subjectivists or not, we need to realize that theorizing about free will needs to be divided into two parts corresponding to meta-ethics and normative ethics. Philosophizing about free will would be no more completed by our selecting between compatibilism and incompatibilism than moral philosophizing is completed by selecting among normative theories. In neither case could we ignore the spectrum of meta-level possibilities. We would instead say things like "If *free choice* makes objective sense, I think libertarianism is correct," just as we can say things like "If I believed in any normative system, it would be act utilitarianism." Free will realists would be opposed by a variety of non-realists, who mirror the various moral non-realists such as the emotivists, expressivists, prescriptivists, error theorists, quasi-realists, and so on.

It would be a mistake to demand that free will non-realists provide a comprehensive account of philosophers' use of *free will*, just as it is wrong to think that moral non-realists have to prove that, for example, emotivism or error theory is *the* correct account of moral language. (Moral realists perform a great metaphilosophical coup when they convince moral non-realists that they must provide semantic analyses of moral language before non-realism is acceptable.) Free will non-realists can argue that *free will* is a moral concept, without having to claim that 'the meaning' of *free will* can be analyzed according to just one pattern. Philosophers' *free will* talk may be as semantically pluralistic as moral language in general is and as resistant to systematic analysis. This is no objection to non-realism, given that ontology is one issue and linguistics another.

9

Hume's Principle:
The Subjectivity of Moral
Responsibility and Free Will

In this chapter I use the Humean principle that one cannot deduce a moral conclusion from a set of non-moral premises (*Treatise*, III, I, I) to support the subjectivity of moral responsibility and free will. The Humean principle is one of the important intermediary principles that goes into Philosophy as Continuous with Science to support the sort of naturalistic view I advocate. If the argument of this chapter is persuasive, we will see that adoption of the Humean principle *by itself* gives very strong reason to accept subjectivism about freedom and responsibility.

In section 1, I define the key terms and defend two important premises: that *moral responsibility* is a moral concept and that subjectivism of moral responsibility strongly supports moral non-realism generally. In section 2, I argue that if we accept the Humean principle, we must conclude that ascriptions of *moral responsibility* cannot be true. On the premise that if ascriptions of *moral responsibility* cannot be true, neither can ascriptions using other moral terms, it follows that the Humean principle entails the general doctrine of moral non-realism. In section 3, I argue that if we accept the Humean principle, we must hold that *free will* is a moral concept. If we add this premise to the conclusion of the previous argument, the defender of the Humean principle is committed to holding that ascriptions of *free choice* cannot be true.

Because the argument of this chapter is somewhat complex, it may be helpful to outline it explicitly:

1. *Moral responsibility* is a moral concept (from section 1).
2. If we accept Hume's principle, then we must believe that ascriptions of *moral responsibility* can be neither true nor false (from section 2).

3. If ascriptions of *moral responsibility* can be neither true nor false, then ascriptions of moral concepts in general can be neither true nor false (from section 1).
4. If we accept Hume's principle, then we must believe that *free will* is a moral concept (from section 3).
5. Therefore, if we accept Hume's principle, then we must believe that ascriptions of *free will* can be neither true nor false (from steps 2–4).
6. Therefore, if we accept Hume's principle, then we must believe that ascriptions of *moral responsibility* can be neither true nor false and that ascriptions of *free will* can be neither true nor false (from steps 2 and 5).

1. Defining the Key Terms

Although the subject of moral realism is extremely complex and has been widely discussed in recent years, a minimal characterization will suffice for my purposes. Moral realism asserts that there are some moral truths— that is, some moral judgments are true. Moral non-realism can be understood as moral realism's negation—that is, there are no moral truths. I divide moral non-realists into two sorts: error theorists such as J. L. Mackie (1977), who believe that all moral judgments are false, and those who think, as A. J. Ayer (1952) does, that moral judgments are neither true nor false.

Consider next the concept *moral responsibility*. Many philosophers writing about free will have recognized that *moral responsibility* is a moral concept, because to say that persons are morally responsible for their actions is to say that they are *legitimately* (Glover, 1970, 19) or *appropriately* (Fischer, 1986B, 12) subject to being held accountable for their behavior. Bruce Waller captures the moral character of *moral responsibility* nicely: "One is *morally* RESPONSIBLE for an act to the degree that it is morally right that one receive special benefit or detriment for it. Moral responsibility involves a moral judgment of what is *fair*: is it fair to treat a person in a special manner because of this act?" (1990, 35). William Frankena suggests: "It seems to me, to say that X was responsible for Y is to say something like: 'It would be right to hold X responsible for Y and to blame or otherwise punish him'" (1973, 72).

I endorse the theme expressed by these philosophers by adopting the following definition for use in this chapter: "*Subject S is morally responsible for act A*" means "*It would be morally right to hold S responsible for A.*" In this definition the idea of being morally responsible is cashed out in terms of the explicit moral notion of the rightness of receiving a certain sort of treatment.

In correspondence, Alfred Mele interestingly objects to my definition: He points out that a utilitarian could imagine cases where it is morally right to hold persons responsible for unintentional acts they perform even though those persons are not morally responsible for them. In such cases the definiens would be true and the definiendum false; so my definition is biased against utilitarians.

One response to Mele would be to concede that my definition is biased against utilitarians but to reply that because *moral responsibility* is a deontological concept that utilitarians find difficult, it is reasonable that its definition should appear biased against them. A second response would be that by giving the counter-example the utilitarian has lapsed into paradox. To be successful the objection requires that moral responsibility lies over and above what is most utile—something that deontologists believe, but not something that utilitarians can maintain consistently. If utilitarians believe that it can be right to hold persons responsible for actions we do not *typically* believe they are responsible for, then utilitarians should consistently espouse their radical theory and maintain that persons are really morally responsible for those actions in those instances. If we adopt a radical theory of when it is right to hold persons responsible, we should adopt a correspondingly radical theory of moral responsibility. If utilitarians do so, the counter-example no longer works.

Because *moral responsibility* is a moral concept, if anyone is morally responsible for anything then there are some moral truths, which is to say that moral realism is true. Contrapositively, if moral non-realism is true, then no one is morally responsible for anything. Importantly for this chapter, because *moral responsibility* is a paradigm of a moral concept, if we adopt a subjectivist interpretation of that term in either the Mackie or Ayer form, we will be strongly committed to adopting the general doctrine of moral non-realism. (This type of subjectivist interpretation would be different from what a hard determinist or No-Free-Will-Either-Way theorist would say about moral responsibility. Because such thinkers believe that the concept makes good sense, even if we fail to be responsible, they are not committed to the general doctrine of moral non-realism. I owe this point to Bruce Waller.) The inference from subjectivism re- garding moral responsibility to the general doctrine of moral non-realism is not deductively valid, but I cannot imagine grounds for treating *moral responsibility* subjectively while treating other moral concepts realisti- cally. So, in lieu of seeing some strong argument to the contrary, I con- clude that if we treat *moral responsibility* subjectively, we are committed to moral non-realism.

Next, consider the famous passage from Hume's *Treatise*, Book III, part I, section I:

> In every system of morality, which I have hitherto met with, I have always remark'd, that the author proceeds for some time in the ordinary way of reasoning, and establishes the being of a God, or makes observations con- cerning human affairs; when of a sudden I am surpriz'd to find, that instead of the usual copulations of propositions, *is*, and *is not*, I meet with no propo- sition that is not connected with an *ought*, or an *ought not*. This change is imperceptible; but is, however, of the last consequence. For as this *ought*, or *ought not*, expresses some new relation or affirmation, 'tis necessary that it shou'd be observ'd and explained; and at the same time that a rea- son should be given, for what seems altogether inconceivable, how this new relation can be a deduction from others, which are entirely different from it. But as authors do not commonly use this precaution, I shall pre- sume to recommend it to the readers; and am persuaded, that this small attention wou'd subvert all the vulgar systems of morality, and let us see, that the distinction of vice and virtue is not founded merely on the rela- tions of objects, nor is perceiv'd by reason. (1968, 469–70)

To use the Humean principle that moral statements cannot be deduced from or entailed by sets of non-moral statements, I need to say how I shall understand it. Let us focus on entailment. There is a way of under- standing *entailment* that provides a cheap proof of the Humean principle but robs it of philosophical interest. This would be by understanding the concept in a purely definitional way, so that it will be true that statements couched in one vocabulary cannot entail statements couched in another unless the relevant vocabulary of the former is definitionally equivalent to ('semantically reducible to') the vocabulary of the latter. On this view of entailment, no statement of, for example, biology is ever entailed by statements of physics unless there are 'meaning postulates' that explic- itly connect the two.

I shall not interpret the Humean principle simply to reject the entailment of moral statements by non-moral statements in this definitional way. Hume's principle has interest if we see it as relevant to meta-ethics, not simply as a point about language. But to apply a purely definitional interpretation to his principle would rob it of this meta-ethical force. For example, to say that no statements of physics entail (in this definitional sense) statements of biology would provide no reason to think that biological facts have a different ontological basis than do the facts of physics. By making the Humean principle too easily true we trivialize it and undo the point of talking about it.

For this reason I adopt a possible-worlds interpretation of *entailment* that gives the Humean principle some meta-ethical force:

> Statement 1 (S1) entails Statement 2 (S2) just in case: (a) (S1) and (S2) are both truth-valued, and (b) In any possible world in which (S1) is true, (S2) is true.

On this view of entailment we can say that "This box is blue all over" entails "This box is not red all over" because there is no possible world where the former is true and the latter is false, without needing to supply the connecting premise that nothing is both blue all over and red all over. Likewise, using this sense of *entailment* would not beg the question against the objector to the Humean principle who believes that non-moral statements might entail moral statements without the need of extra premises to bridge the semantic gap—for example, that "This is an act of deliberate cruelty" entails "This act is wrong."

2. Why Hume's Principle Implies That Ascriptions of *Moral Responsibility* Cannot Be True

The argument in this section shows how a set of non-moral statements will entail a moral conclusion—contrary to the Humean principle—unless we deny that moral responsibility ascriptions can be true. Thus, if we wish to accept the Humean principle we must hold that moral responsibility ascriptions cannot be true.

I begin with a premise that *appears* to be a definitional truth about a moral concept and, hence, is not itself a statement in normative ethics:

(1) (a) "S is morally responsible for S's (actual) doing of act A" entails (b) "S does A."

Statement (1) is expressed somewhat pedantically to obviate irrelevant objections. First, it may be objected that S may be morally responsible for T's drowning without S doing *anything* (perhaps S should have done something to prevent T's drowning). This may be true, but T's drowning is not something S actually does. Second, S may be morally responsible for U's death if S hires T who murders U. But in this case S is morally responsible for U's murder, not for S's committing of the murder, inasmuch as S did not commit the murder.

One might object to my calling (1) *non-moral* by saying that it is a moral premise that expresses a normative view about when it is morally permissible to hold persons accountable for their actions. For instance, one might say, "What is to prevent us from *holding* S morally responsible for A even if S did not do A? Only our belief that it would be *morally wrong* to do so. Hence, (1) rests not on the meaning of *moral responsibility* but on our moral judgment, thus it is a normative claim."

This objection fails because it conflates two questions: (i) "*Is* S morally responsible for A?" and (ii) "How do we *feel about* holding S morally responsible for an act that S did not perform?" The only way that these questions might seem to be asking the same thing is if we are convinced that there is no answer to (i) except our answer to (ii), which would be to deny that moral responsibility ascriptions may be objectively true. But to resist my argument in this way would be to concede the substantive claim of this section: that defenders of the Humean principle must deny that ascriptions of *moral responsibility* are ever true. So this is not a strategically apt way to resist my argument.

Given this fact about the dialectic of my argument, we are left with every reason to suppose that moral responsibility *for* performing acts is logically dependent on performing those acts. We cannot be causally or legally responsible *for* doing A unless we do A. Likewise, it would seem, we cannot be morally responsible for doing A unless we do A. The question asked in (ii) amounts to the question of what we think about holding persons morally responsible for acts for which they are not morally responsible. To *that* question several answers are possible depending on our normative views, but the fact that a moral disagreement is possible concerning (ii) gives no reason to think that statement (1) is a normative claim.

Suppose next that S does not do A. Then we may add to the derivation the empirical, non-moral negation of (b):

(2) "Not (S does A)."

From (1) and (2) we deduce the negation of (a):

(3) "Not (S is morally responsible for S's [actual] doing of act A)."

Because S did not do A, S is not morally responsible for S's actual doing of A, inasmuch as there *was* no S's actual doing of A.

Now, on my definition of *moral responsibility* provided above, (3) means:

(4) "Not (It would be morally right to hold S responsible for S's [actual] doing of act A)."

Step (4) almost takes us to the moral claim that I seek to derive, but it does not quite make it. To an unmeticulous reader, (4) might seem equivalent to (6) "It would be morally wrong to hold S responsible for S's (actual) doing of A." But the inference from (4) to (6) is invalid. What if there are no rights or wrongs concerning the morality of holding persons responsible? Statement (4) does not logically imply (6), because (4) is consistent with a statement that implies that (6) is false: (4') "It is neither morally right nor morally wrong to hold S responsible for S's (actual) doing of act A." (Compare: "Not [This pen is blue]" does not imply "This pen is a non-blue color," because it is logically possible that physical objects are not colored at all.)

To complete the derivation we need a premise that takes us from (4) to (6) by eliminating the above rejoinder. The denial of (4') should do the trick: "It is not the case that it is neither morally right nor morally wrong to hold S responsible for S's (actual) doing of act A." This rejection of moral non-realism, when instanced to moral responsibility, can be stated more directly as an affirmation of moral realism applied to moral responsibility:

(5) "It is either morally right or morally wrong to hold S responsible for S's (actual) doing of act A."

Because (5) is an application of moral realism to moral responsibility, it is not a moral claim. Although it makes a claim *about* ethics, it is not a claim *in* normative ethics. But once we add (5) to the derivation, we can conclude from (4) and (5) by disjunctive syllogism:

(6) "Therefore, it would be morally wrong to hold S responsible for S's (actual) doing of act A."

The *apparent* result of our derivation is that we have deduced a statement in normative ethics from a combination of non-moral premises. Statement (1) is true by definition, (2) is an empirical claim, (3) logically follows from (1) and (2), (4) follows from (3) by definition, and (6) follows from (4) with the addition of the meta-ethical, non-normative claim (5). It looks as if the Humean principle stands refuted.

How might someone who accepts the Humean principle resist its refutation? Adopting moral non-realism of either the Ayer or Mackie variety will suffice by giving us a way to reject (5) and stop the derivation at that point. But doing this, of course, would be tantamount to accepting my thesis that the Humean principle implies that ascriptions of *moral responsibility* cannot be true. If we apply an Ayer-type moral non-realism to moral responsibility, we can reject (5) and block the inference from (4) to (6). In addition, on this tack the derivation cannot even get started, because (1) will be seen to be false because (a) has no truth-value and cannot entail anything.

If we block the derivation by applying a Mackie-type error theory to moral responsibility, we also shall conclude that moral responsibility ascriptions cannot be true. Unlike Ayer-type theories, a Mackie-type theory would not permit us to say that (1) is false. If we say that moral judgments are always false, we would have to accept (1) as vacuously true because (a) would be false for all S's and all A's. But the derivation still remains blocked at (5). If all moral judgments are false, then it will always be false to say that it is right to hold S responsible for A AND it will always be false to say that it is wrong to hold S responsible for A. Thus, on a Mackie-type view, (5) is a disjunction with two false disjuncts and is false. The important thing to emphasize is that whether we apply an Ayer-type or Mackie-type theory to moral responsibility in order to save the Humean principle from refutation, we have committed ourselves to the view that no one is morally responsible for anything.

3. Why Hume's Principle Implies That *Free Choice* Is a Moral Concept

The argument of this section will look like this. Any defender of the Humean principle who believes as I do that *moral responsibility* is a moral concept is committed to holding that no set of non-moral statements about agents' choices can entail the moral conclusion that those agents are morally responsible for their choices. Thus, *if* we can specify a set of apparently non-moral statements that entail that agents *are* morally responsible for their choices, then the defender of the Humean principle must say that at least one member of the entailing set is moral. I shall show how to specify such a set of statements, and among that set the only plausible candidate for being moral is the ascription of *free choice*. So, the defender of the Humean principle must conclude that ascriptions of *free choice* are moral judgments. Finally, I argued in section 2 that the Humean principle implies that ascriptions of *moral responsibility* cannot be true. Because moral responsibility is a paradigm of a moral property, I conclude that the Humean principle implies moral non-realism. So if defenders of the Humean principle must hold that ascriptions of *free will* are moral claims, then they must hold that ascriptions of *free choice* cannot be true.

I begin the argument by trying to collect a set of statements that entails the moral claim (M): "S is morally responsible for choice C that produces act A." The most important statement of the set, which I shall argue must be moral, is (F): "S freely makes choice C." Although compatibilists and incompatibilists differ notoriously over the truth-conditions of (F), still (F) is the most important contributing condition for (M).

Statement (F) by itself does not entail (M), because if S does not fully understand what choice C is, then S might not be responsible for it. So we need to add a second statement (K): "S fully and accurately knows what choice is being made." Perhaps there are possible worlds where (F) and (K) are true and (M) is false, because S fails to understand the consequences of the action that C produces and this ignorance absolves S of moral responsibility. To handle this possibility let us add to (F) and (K) statement (A): "S fully and accurately foresees the consequences of the action that choice C will produce." These three statements might appear to eliminate all of the 'loopholes' by which S might fail to be morally responsible for C, but there may be others. Suppose that we are attracted to Susan Wolf's claim that agents cannot be morally responsible for wrong acts they did not (or could not) know to be wrong (1990, 37–38). In this case, we add to the entailing set statement (N): "S knows the moral nature of A."

A pattern has emerged. For any unfulfilled condition that an objector cites to block the entailment of (M) by the rest, I add to the set a statement explicitly indicating that the additional condition has been met. Although I cannot foresee all possible factors that might be parlayed into objections, I have found a strategy to neutralize them. Thus, there are inductive grounds for thinking that a set of apparently non-moral statements such as (F), (K), (A), (N), and any others required to block further objections will entail the moral conclusion (M).

Given the entailment, the defender of the Humean principle has to conclude that some member of the entailing set is really a moral claim. Statements (K) and (A) are unquestionably empirical and non-moral. Statement (N), as someone who adopts Wolf's view understands it, expresses a claim about S's cognitive state and is non-moral for that reason, despite the fact that it takes morality as its object of cognition. Although I cannot be certain about what the other possible members of the entailing set might look like without seeing them, because they will be generated in the same way that (K), (A), and (N) were, there is inductive reason to think that, if generated, they would be empirical and non-moral.

This leaves (F) as the best candidate for being moral. For consider this: If the defender of the Humean principle accepts my argument so far and has to say that one among (F), (K), (A), and (N) is moral, which seems the most likely? Statement (F), given the notorious, murky record of philosophical debate over the 'true' nature of free will and the arguments provided in the last chapter, seems the clear choice.

Let me consider several objections that the defender of the Humean principle might pose to the derivation just provided. First, an objector might say that: (i) The Humean principle is true, (ii) the set of statements such as (F), (K), (A), and (N) simply *are* all non-moral, and, hence, (iii) that set of statements *cannot* entail a moral statement such as (M). So the derivation *must* fail, even if no reason can be given to demonstrate why it fails. This is a non-reply. Simply to stipulate that all of the statements in the entailing set are non-moral is question-begging.

Second, the objector might think that there *is* some good reason why the derivation fails but plead inability to specify what that reason is. This objection also may be dismissed. Third, the objector, perhaps without realizing it, might be appealing to the definitional notion of entailment rather than the possible-worlds interpretation and, in effect, be drawing our attention to the fact that there is no explicit semantic link between the entailing set and (M). As noted in section 1, we expect more from the defender of the Humean principle than the recognition of this boring fact. Fourth, an objector might accept the derivation but deny that (M) *is* a moral claim and, thus, deny that any member of the entailing set needs to be moral. But there are the reasons already given for thinking that *moral responsibility* is not only a moral concept but a paradigm of a moral concept.

A fifth objection would be as follows. Suppose the defender of the Humean principle endorses a Mackie-type moral non-realism and believes that the reason why the set of apparently factual statements cannot entail (M) is that (M) cannot be true. (Perhaps the objector has come to deny that [M] can be true because of reasons like those rehearsed in the previous section.) Ironically, perhaps the fact that the Humean principle implies moral non-realism may seem to defeat my attempt to show that free-will ascriptions are moral claims.

This objection can be rebutted. One cannot say that simply because (S2) is false in all possible worlds, (S1) cannot entail (S2). For example, if (S2) is "B and not B," then (S1) may entail (S2), although the only way that (S1) could entail (S2) is if (S1) is also false in all possible worlds. So, if moral responsibility ascriptions are necessarily false (which follows from Mackie's error theory and my premise that moral-responsibility ascriptions are moral claims), then it does not follow that they cannot be entailed by the seemingly factual set. They may be. Instead, what follows from a Mackie-type view is that if moral-responsibility ascriptions are entailed by a set of statements, then either some individual member of that set must be false in all possible worlds, or in each possible world some member or other must be false, although not necessarily the same member in each world. Statement (F)'s being false in all possible worlds remains the most likely candidate.

Here is one complication regarding the fifth objection. An objector could apply an Ayer-type view of moral non-realism regarding (M), saying that (M) is neither true nor false, rather than false in all possible worlds. Thus, (M) cannot be entailed by the other statements, given my definition of *entailment*. So (F) cannot be shown to be a moral claim by my argument, which depends on (M)'s having a truth-value.

Several points can be offered in reply. First, this objection still endorses my contention that moral responsibility ascriptions cannot be true. But moral responsibility is the principal reason for caring about the free will problem in the first place. So the fifth objection represents at most a Pyrrhic victory against my overall view. Second, taking an Ayer-like view of (M) may enable us to resist my specific argument that free will ascriptions are moral, but it gives no reason to think that the conclusion of the argument is false. If anything, if we endorse an Ayer-type moral non-realism for (M), we should be sympathetic regarding the plausibility of applying an Ayer-type view to (F). Third, an Ayer-type moral non-realism may be less satisfactory than an error theory on general grounds. Fourth, if we were to adopt Ayer's view that moral judgments lack truth-values, we probably should drop the first condition of our definition of *entailment* and offer a revised definition that permits entailment to hold even where not all of the statements in the relation are truth-valued (as in Castañeda, 1974 and 1975). On a suitably revised definition it may turn out that only statements that are false (or statements that lack truth-values) can *entail* non-truth-valued conclusions.

4. Conclusion

I have argued that accepting the Humean principle, given the premise that moral-responsibility ascriptions are moral claims, commits us to a non-realist interpretation of moral-responsibility ascriptions. Since moral-responsibility ascriptions are paradigms of moral claims, we would then be committed to the general doctrine of moral non-realism. I have also argued that holding the Humean principle commits us to viewing ascriptions of *free will* as moral claims and, given what went before, to thinking that these ascriptions cannot be true. I have indicated some places where there is room to resist these conclusions, but I doubt that there is very much.

This chapter constructs a logical progression from Hume's remark about moral language to the thesis of moral non-realism to the doctrine of non-realism in the free will problem. I claim not that Hume 'should' have reasoned this way but that the progression expands Hume's principle in what I think is a natural (and naturalistic) way. Some friends of the Humean principle might be surprised to think that it can be extended all the way to free will, while others might have recognized the connection all along. To those who think the Humean principle is false because we can derive "ought" statements from "is" statements, or who reject it because they eschew the fact/value distinction altogether, I have no reply. The Humean principle and the fact/value distinction probably stand or fall together. Both views are examples of intermediate-level principles that, even if they are capable of being true or false, are never proved nor disproved in philosophy. Instead, they constitute a distinctive approach to philosophy.

10
Conclusion

1. Where We Are

In this book I have examined the connection between metaphilosophy and one specific philosophical problem. Regarding that problem, I think that the most-likely-to-be-true picture of what exists contains neither free choices nor moral responsibility, irrespective of whether human choices are determined. I think that my subjectivist variety of non-realism, assuming the metaphilosophy and intermediate-level principles that I accept, is more plausible than any of the familiar free will theories. But subjectivist non-realism by its own lights cannot support itself decisively. This is due to the evaluative nature of metaphilosophies and the role that metaphilosophies play in the justification of free will theories.

Even if we reject subjectivism, we cannot show any free will theory to be more plausible than the rest. The plausibility of any free will theory depends on the adoption of a supporting metaphilosophy and intermediate-level principles and the avoidance of meta-level views that would undermine it. The 'right' metaphilosophy can make a free will theory, and the 'wrong' one can break it. But philosophers cannot show that their metaphilosophies are superior to other metaphilosophies irrespective of what we want to accomplish by philosophizing, because metaphilosophies depend on our desires-for-philosophy. Even if subjectivism is false, no one can show which desires-for-philosophy are 'best.' It follows that no free will theory can be shown to be best. By this I mean that for any free will theory T we select (which is supported by metaphilosophy M1), we can adopt a conflicting metaphilosophy M2 that has just as much claim to being provable as M1 has—that is, *none*—and shows that T's competitor is better than T. I take this to be a fairly radical type of unprovability. Thus, argumentation in the free will problem depends on non-truth-valued factors in a way that is not widely recognized. The conclusions philosophers reach in other areas of philosophy do also, although I have not argued the case.

Although the argument of this book is conceptual, its result is to psychologize the free will problem in a certain way. It is not that philosophical notions such as *validity* and *warrant* describe mental processes in the way that 'psychologistic' philosophers have said that logic represents the laws of thought. Rather, we find philosophical theories to be warranted due to our metaphilosophical preferences, which depend on our values and cannot be supported except by appeal to our feelings. 'Psychology,' in the sense of these psychological states, plays the decisive role in the free will debate, even if the concepts of philosophy are not psychological.

According to this thesis, the key to understanding the free will debate is to see its dependence on motivation. In "Philosophy in America Today" (1982, 221), Richard Rorty claims that although analytic philosophers are extremely *clever*, they do not live up to their reputations for being *wise*. By *wise* Rorty means possessing great learning across a broad humanistic spectrum. The point that I would make is that although analytic philosophers are extremely clever, many of them do not live up to their reputations for being *unbiased*. Philosophers often decide where they want to end before they begin their arguments, rather than follow the arguments wherever they lead. Most philosophers turn their impressive analytical abilities to the task of validating philosophical views that they accept prephilosophically. Platonism, for example, is endorsed by some philosophers because of its usefulness in supporting the doctrine of Original Sin (Philosophy as Underpinning Religion) and by others because of its usefulness in arguing for collective responsibility by those who want to promote compensatory justice (Philosophy as Praxis).

With notable exceptions, most of the published work designed to contribute to philosophers' understanding of the free will problem tends to be narrow, highly focused, and technical and to work within an established framework of assumptions. Given the assumptions that these authors make, their work is rigorous, highly impressive, even awe-inspiring. I include the treatments by G. E. Moore, J. L. Austin, Roderick Chisholm, Keith Lehrer, and John Martin Fischer on "could have done otherwise"; the debate over Harry Frankfurt's (1969) non-intervening, but would-have-intervened-had-you-begun-to-choose-differently remote controller; and the discussion of Peter van Inwagen's (1983) consequence argument for incompatibilism.

Although this type of free will writing pays dividends in terms of precision, it has disadvantages. First, we may lose sight of the philosophical forest for the technical trees. Second, and following from the first, we may collect psychological consolation at the expense of candor. By submerging ourselves in the nuances of theories, we may avert our attention from the big, scary questions. Attention to detail can be an exercise in bad faith when it uses up our time and energies so that we do not bother to question whether what we are trying to do is possible. Meticulous precision can enable us to remain happy and engaged at the expense of averting our eyes from the disturbing big picture. This is to be expected if our work in free will is motivated in the sense described.

To say that metaphilosophies are the products of motivation is not to say that we are always aware of the motivation. Few philosophers who are influenced by the non-truth-tracking metaphilosophies say: "Let truth be damned; I want philosophy above all else to be intellectually interesting (or to enhance human well-being, or to support other areas of intellectual life that I care about)." If we were to consciously proclaim this, we would reduce our ability to use philosophy to serve these other goals. Motivation is usually more subtle than this. Our desires for various goals influence our meta-level views without our explicit recognition of our motivation. In addition, our recognition of the motivational causes of our selection of metaphilosophies is obscured by the fact that in many cases we are motivated in different directions that correspond to different metaphilosophies.

2. Philosophical Consequences

How should we respond as philosophers if we accept my thesis about the unprovability of free will theories due to the unprovability of metaphilosophy? An obvious question to ask is whether the thesis (NP) "*No free will theory is provable*" supports the nihilistic claim (NT) "*No free will theory is true.*" If we believe that truth entails provability, as verificationists and pragmatists do, we will think that (NP) entails (NT). If we are strong realists, we will deny that (NP) supports (NT) at all, because the defining mark of realism is the belief that truth outruns knowledge and justification. If we are somewhere in the middle, we might take an intermediate stand on how much (NP) supports (NT). Because verificationism seems to me to be a poor method for tracking truth—verificationism is a method that those who adopt Philosophy as Worldview Construction would do well to avoid—I doubt that (NP) lends any support to (NT). But verificationism, in one form or another, is unlikely to die off, as we have seen in this century. In addition, because verificationism is such a powerful philosophical tool, it serves various metaphilosophical motivations and derives support from the irrefutable character of the metaphilosophies it serves.

I have argued that although some theory concerning free will is true (the subjectivist view of part II), we cannot prove which theory it is. This type of conclusion may be unsettling to non-philosophers, but it should look familiar to philosophers. My argument simply adds an extra dimension of under-determination to the generally recognized under-determination of theories by their data: the fact that free will theories are under-determined also by meta-level considerations, especially by our desires-for-philosophy. There is no reason why we *must* draw dire philosophical implications from this view, because we could simply accept this as one more limit to philosophical 'knowledge' and resolve to continue to work with that recognition. We might say: "Here are my proposals regarding metaphilosophy, intermediate-level philosophical principles, and specific free will theories. I cannot prove the package is best, and I cannot prove that you should care about the values my package endorses. But see how nicely they fit together. Consider my view and see how you like it."

We could make other responses. A pessimistic response would be that all free will theories are hopeless wastes of time, and, by parity of reasoning, that any other philosophical theory that is likewise dependent on meta-level views is also. Another response would be more tolerant, seeing the debate over free will theories as does an aesthete who sees debates over artistic merit as neither provable nor truth-tracking but as potentially principled and worth thinking about. Richard Rorty's ironist, who "spends her time worrying about the possibility that she has been . . . taught to play the wrong language game" (1989, 75) might agree with the conclusion of this book but would recoil at the method I used to get there.

I want to claim two advantages for free will subjectivism over all varieties of free will realism. First, I showed in chapter 6 how my subjectivist free will non-realism differs from the non-realism of hard determinism and No-Free-Will-Either-Way Theory. Although all three views agree that free will does not exist, they reach their conclusions in very different ways. Hard determinists believe that free will would exist except for the unhappy fact of determinism. No-Free-Will-Either-Way theorists agree with the negative theses of both the hard determinists and the libertarians, thereby also assuming that free will is a coherent idea that we unhappily fail to enjoy. Given the routes these thinkers take to their conclusions, it is easy to see how they would feel a sense of regret that we subjectivists do not feel. Subjectivism holds that this regret is based on a confusion. So I suspect that free will non-realism is a cheerier position for subjectivists than it is for the hard determinists or the No-Free-Will-Either-Way theorists.

Second, realists assign a great value to our having free will, thereby suggesting that there is also a great disvalue to our *not* having it. The most forthright example I know of is Robert Kane's (1996) view, cited in chapter 8, that free will is necessary for: (1) deserving ascriptions of *moral responsibility*, (2) being suitable objects of reactive attitudes, (3) deserving praise for our achievements, (4) having the capacity to love and be loved, and having (5) genuine creativity, (6) true individuality, (7) autonomy, and (8) dignity or self-worth. Not all free will realists will agree with Kane that all of these things require free will, but most agree with much of Kane's list.

If we step back for a moment, we see that some *extremely desirable* human traits are being held hostage to a risky metaphysical thesis: the existence of free will in the libertarian, compatibilist, or Free-Will-Either-Way form. Realizing that free will realists believe I lose these traits if I do not have free will is enough to make me feel mildly squeamish in their presence. (I include even the hard determinists and No-Free-Will-Either-Way theorists, who are typically naturalists and in many ways my philosophical allies.) Suppose an incompatibilist becomes convinced by an article in *Science* that determinism holds for the macroscopic world, including persons' choices. Then by that incompatibilist's lights, I lose all the good things that require free will. This chilling sort of chauvinism strikes me as on a par with other philosophical chauvinisms. In the philosophy of mind it has been argued that we cannot be persons if we are not made up of hydrocarbons (Materialism) or if we fail to have nonphysical minds (Cartesian dualism). In normative ethics, if we think that morality requires God, then we are committed to thinking with Dostoevski that morality is in jeopardy of God's nonexistence. If morality requires objective moral truths of any sort, then morality depends on the questionable thesis of moral realism. Compatibilists and Free-Will-Either-Way theorists try to make free will realism less perilous by making free will invulnerable to determinism. But even these theories put valuable human characteristics at risk to the subjectivist arguments raised in this book.

Free will realists could make several replies to my charge that they have put too much of what we care about at risk. First, they could insist that although they put much at risk, we should not worry because they have the right view for vindicating free will. This response, given the history of the free will problem, would appear to be false bravado. Second, they could compartmentalize their thinking, admitting that as a metaphysical problem free will cannot be settled but claiming that the problem is to be ignored when we deal with our students, spouses, and children. By my lights, this separation does not seem very philosophical.

I recommend a different strategy that will allow us to integrate our thinking about the free will problem and our desire to continue to impute to persons autonomy, dignity, and the rest. In doing so I rely on the subjectivist notion of the autonomy of desire, which is just an application of the fact/value distinction. Suppose we deny the chauvinism implicit in free will realism by saying that if we desire to continue to view ourselves as morally responsible, autonomous, and worthy of dignity, we may. If free will and moral responsibility can be nothing more than a matter of how we feel about ourselves, and if there can be no metaphysical prohibitions as to how we may feel, then we may continue to see ourselves in those terms even as we explicitly recognize free will as subjective. A sentiment-based view of free will is not held hostage to the factual thesis of free will realism. This is parallel to a sentiment-based view of ethics that takes right and wrong to be the way that humans feel about actions—without requiring support from moral realism. We can, if we like, see free will and morality as based on sentiments; once we quit trying to 'ground' these entities in metaphysical facts, we are not the worse for it as philosophers.

3. Consequences for Persons

At a personal level, I am not discouraged by the doctrine of the subjectivity of free will and moral responsibility. The naturalism that I reach via my meta-level views contains sufficient resources to support what I care about by way of action and morality. Without including God, souls, immortality, Platonic moral truths, naturalistic moral properties, and realistic free will of any variety, we can have a worldview where human welfare counts as much as we want it to count. Even if we explicitly see philosophy as an attempt to make the intellectual world safe for moral decency (Rorty, 1989, chapter 1), we do not need these props. Moral feelings, although *contingent* in Rorty's sense, are widely enough shared that most persons who do not suffer abysmal environments can come to treat other persons with benevolence—without needing either the actual existence of these theological and philosophical entities or the belief in them. (A cynic would suggest that these props have not heretofore contributed greatly to human well-being.) We do not need to believe in objective moral truth to accept Confucius's doctrine not to do things to others that we do not want them to do to us. We do not need to believe in free will to run a legal system. We do not need a justification of reactive attitudes to be kind.

Mark Bernstein suggests that without these historically powerful metaphysical beliefs, philosophers as persons may find it more difficult to stand firm against what we believe is immoral. This may be true, but I am doubtful. I have recognized no less decency among philosophers who deny the existence of God, free will, and objective morality than among those who are realists, although I admit this is just an impression. Another reader of the manuscript suggests that philosophical theories such as subjectivism might harm a society's morality. This is also possible, but I would suggest that: (1) The moral decline of a society (at least contemporary America) is the result of large, non-rational, causal forces where intellectual factors play no significant role. Consider the decline of religion, which many persons believe has affected collective morality. Simplifying to a proximate cause, the main reason is that children are receiving less training in religion. This seems to me to be due to various sociological factors, such as more single-parent homes, more divorce, longer work weeks for parents, more mothers in the workforce, and more competition from other directions for children's attention. The fact that, for example, J. L. Mackie (1982) wrote a brilliant book against arguments for the existence of God is not important. (2) To the extent that reflective thought affects public morality at all, most individuals get most of their intellectual insight from imbibing the most mindless aspects of the ambient intellectual environment—peers who are no more reflective than they are, television, movies, sports, and lyrics from popular songs—not from reading philosophical work. So I doubt that much of an argument can be made that philosophers and other intellectuals have a moral obligation to prop up the moral props. Intellectuals might have a greater influence than I think they do, but I suspect the belief that they do is a vanity of intellectuals.

I grant that if we accept a naturalism devoid of moral responsibility, moral objectivism, and free will, we will be less tempted to try to *prove* to our students that sympathy (or the desire to do one's duty) *should* be the basis of morality rather than another sentiment such as the will to power, self-love, or even general maliciousness. But such arguments never generate warranted conviction anyway (moral realism being unprovable), and to the extent that they garner unwarranted conviction, they are doubtful to their believers, for it is always possible to see through them dimly. It is better to do away with such arguments honestly. There is no point in propounding mysteries.

I have emphasized the desire-based, willful nature of human reason: We end up in our theoretical reasoning largely where we want to end up. This is parallel to the desire-based character of morality. Morality depends on feelings, attitudes, and sentiments: "We are ourselves the ultimate and irrefutable arbiters of value. . . . It is we who create value and our desires which confer value" (Russell, 1925, 16). According to such a view, which was also held by Sartre and Nietzsche, moral realism of even the most atheological sort is similar to religious authoritarianism in a crucial respect. With both religious authoritarianism and moral realism we try to ignore our role in determining morality by shunting the determination of right and wrong onto some reality that is independent of our wills. The trouble is, we often see through that attempt. We might as well acknowledge our role and quit trying to ground morality in 'moral facts.' Seen from this perspective, moral realism is an escape from freedom—namely, our plight of having to decide what is right and wrong.

But how should we *feel* as persons if we accept the theses of this book? Philosophy as Continuous with Science tries to address philosophical questions without worrying about how the answers make us feel. If the picture I have sketched regarding free will and moral responsibility contributes to human well-being, so much the better. But in all areas where there is a conflict between truth-tracking and welfare, *for the philosopher*, the former trumps the latter. The case is likewise regarding the other aims for philosophy held by the other metaphilosophies. If our attempt to construct the most probable view of what exists results in interesting conversation, speaks usefully to the moral dimension of human existence, or provides underpinnings for other areas that we care about, so much the better. But the enhancement of these other aims is not what philosophy is *for*, according to Philosophy as Continuous with Science.

This is not to say that *as a person* the philosopher who accepts this metaphilosophy 'should' always prefer truth to all other goals. Truth is only one goal among many. It follows that it is an open question whether the philosopher who accepts this metaphilosophy is logically committed to being philosophical. Perhaps, all things considered, philosophers 'should' be philosophical only sometimes.

I grant that I can become discouraged to think that: (1) Free will and moral responsibility are merely subjective, and (2) I cannot even collect the satisfaction of thinking that I can prove that I am right about (1). Nonetheless, if we want to derive gratification from (1) and (2), we can without too many psychological hijinks. This may seem somewhat strange, because the metaphilosophy I adopt aims at truth-tracking irrespective of how unconsoling that truth may be. Nonetheless, one can derive consolation through the *process* of reaching a conclusion whose *content* is not all that consoling. Philosophy as Continuous with Science and its negative verdict on free will and moral responsibility might even be more consoling than a metaphilosophy that allows consolation to be a partial goal. Remember Aristotle's suggestion (*Nicomachean Ethics*, Bk. I, Ch. 8) that the best way to obtain pleasure is by aiming at a goal other than pleasure. If we realize that we have stacked the deck in our own favor, then our realization may undermine our conviction. Perhaps non-truth-tracking metaphilosophies can achieve their aims only through self-deception.

Here is a slightly different recipe for optimism. Suppose we adopt a quasi-Aristotelian view of the 'proper functions' of our 'faculties.' Then we could say that if we desire various goals besides collecting beliefs with the best chance of being true (e.g., making interesting conversation, improving the moral fabric of the world, or supporting religion), we should strive for these goals directly using the faculties appropriate to the job. Write literature, join a political party, go to church. But don't misuse your faculty of reason, whose 'proper function' is to track truths, by using it to pursue those other goals that should be sought in other, more appropriate ways. Add to this the Stoic recommendation to reconcile ourselves to the facts, unpleasant though they may be. Suppose we see this ability to accept unhappy truths as a virtue. Finally, add the

Humean idea that logically we can adopt any attitude we like toward any fact. If it is not contrary to reason to prefer the destruction of the world to the scratching of my finger, then it is not contrary to reason to find subjectivism, or our willingness to accept subjectivism, to be happy thoughts.

Putting these three ideas together, we can paint a picture that I find attractive. As philosophers, we try to construct a worldview we think is most likely to be true, while trying the best we can to hold in abeyance other metaphilosophical motivations. Then, as good Stoics, we try to reconcile ourselves to that view, whatever it may be. Finally, we rely on the elasticity of attitudes to respond to those conclusions in such a way as to contribute to the other goals endorsed by the other metaphilosophies —to lift the human spirit, for example, or make the world safe for morality.

Admittedly, there are limitations to this process, and we may have to make some accommodations. For example, if we want to support religion, and our Worldview Construction results are that there is no God, we may need to shift to some religion where atheism is not a problem, or to reinterpret our religion so that its claims do not conflict with our philosophical results. Nonetheless, there are compensating advantages. The practitioners of Philosophy as Continuous with Science can flatter themselves on their willingness to face up to the consequences of their philosophical reasoning, wherever it may lead them. And we could be proud of our ability to accommodate philosophy's distinctive contribution and the other things we want from philosophy. One can find gratification in this.

References

Audi, R. (1986). "Acting for Reasons." *The Philosophical Review* [vol. 95], 511–46.

Austin, J. L. (1970). "A Plea for Excuses." In Austin, *Philosophical Papers*, 175–204. Oxford: Oxford University Press.

Ayer, A. J. (1952). Language, *Truth, and Logic*. New York: Dover.

———. (1954). "Freedom and Necessity." In Ayer, *Philosophical Essays*, 271–84. London: Macmillan.

Bennett, J. (1980). "Accountability." In Van Straaten (1980), 14–47.

Blackburn, S. (1984). *Spreading the Word*. Oxford: Oxford University Press.

Blumenfeld, D. (1988). "Freedom and Mind Control." *American Philosophical Quarterly* [vol. 25], 215–27.

Boyd, R. (1988). "How to Be a Moral Realist." In Sayre-McCord (1988), 181–228.

Brink, D. (1989). *Moral Realism and the Foundations of Ethics*. Cambridge: Cambridge University Press.

Campbell, C. A. (1951). "Is Free Will a Pseudo-Problem?" *Mind* [vol. 60], 446–65.

———. (1957). *On Selfhood and Godhood*. New York: Macmillan.

Campbell, J., and R. Pargetter (1986). "Goodness and Fragility." *American Philosophical Quarterly* [vol. 23], 155–65.

Camus, A. (1955). *The Myth of Sisyphus*. New York: Random House.

Castañeda, H. (1974). *The Structure of Morality*. Springfield, IL: Thomas.

———. (1975). *Thinking and Doing*. Boston: Reidel.

Chisholm, R. (1976). *Person and Object*. LaSalle, IL: Open Court.

Clarke, R. (1992). "A Principle of Rational Explanation?" *The Southern Journal of Philosophy* [vol. 33], 1–12.

———. (1993). "Toward a Credible Agent-Causal Account of Free Will." *Noûs* [vol. 27], 191–203.

Clifford, W. K. (1877). "The Ethics of Belief." In Clifford, *Lectures and Essays* [vol. 2], 163–205. New York: Macmillan.

Cockburn, D. (1992). Review of *The Non-Reality of Free Will* and *Freedom within Reason*. The Philosophical Quarterly [vol. 42], 383–88.

Cornman, J. (1975). *Perception, Common Sense, and Science*. New Haven: Yale University Press.

Dennett, D. (1984). *Elbow Room*. Cambridge: MIT Press.

Dewey, J. (1926). *Experience and Theory*. LaSalle, IL: Open Court.

————. (1948). *Reconstruction in Philosophy*. Boston: Beacon Press.

Double, R. (1988A). "Libertarianism and Rationality." *The Southern Journal of Philosophy* [vol. 26], 431–39. In O'Connor (1995B).

————. (1988B). "What's Wrong with Self-Serving Epistemic Strategies?" *Philosophical Psychology* [vol. 1], 343–50.

————. (1989). "Puppeteers, Hypnotists, and Neurosurgeons." *Philosophical Studies* [vol. 56], 163–73.

————. 1990. "Sayre-McCord on Evaluative Facts." *The Southern Journal of Philosophy* [vol. 28], 165–69.

————. (1991A). "Determinism and the Experience of Freedom." *Pacific Philosophical Quarterly* [vol. 72], 1–8.

————. (1991B). *The Non-Reality of Free Will*. New York: Oxford University Press.

————. (1992). "How Rational Must Free Will Be?" *Metaphilosophy* [vol. 23], 268–78.

————. (1993). "The Principle of Rational Explanation Defended." *The Southern Journal of Philosophy* [vol. 31], 133–42.

————. (1994). "How to Frame the Free Will Problem." *Philosophical Studies* [vol. 75], 149–72.

Drey, W. (1957). *Laws and Explanation in History*. Oxford: Clarendon Press.

Feuer, L. (1959). *Marx and Engels: Basic Writings on Politics and Philosophy*. New York: Doubleday.

Fichte, J. (1956). *The Vocation of Man*. Indianapolis: Bobbs-Merrill.

Fischer, J. M., ed. (1986A). *Moral Responsibility*. Ithaca: Cornell University Press.

————. (1986B). "Van Inwagen on Free Will." *Philosophical Quarterly* [vol. 36], 252–60.

————. (1992). Review of *The Non-Reality of Free Will. Philosophy and Phenomenological Research* [vol. 72], 1004–7.

————. (1994). *The Metaphysics of Free Will*. Oxford: Blackwell.

Flew, A. (1959). "Divine Omniscience and Human Freedom." In A. Flew and A. MacIntyre, eds., *New Essays in Philosophical Theology*, 144–69. London and New York: Macmillan.

Frankena, W. (1973). *Ethics*. 2d ed. Englewood Cliffs, NJ: Prentice-Hall.

Frankfurt, H. (1969). "Alternate Possibilities and Moral Responsibility." *The Journal of Philosophy* [vol. 66], 828–39.

————. (1971). "Freedom of the Will and the Concept of a Person." In Fischer (1986A).

French, P., ed. (1991). *The Spectrum of Responsibility*. New York: St. Martin's.

Gibbard, A. (1990). *Wise Choices, Apt Feelings*. Cambridge: Harvard University Press.

Ginet, C. (1989). "Reasons Explanation of Action: An Incompatibilist Account." In J. Tomberlin, ed., *Philosophy of Mind and Action Theory*, 17–46. Philosophical Perspectives [vol. 3]. Atascadero, CA: Ridgeview.

Glover, J. (1970). *Responsibility*. London: Routledge and Kegan Paul.

Harman, G. (1977). *The Nature of Morality*. New York: Oxford University Press.

Heil, J., ed. (1993). *Rationality, Morality, and Self-Interest*. Lanham, MD: Rowman & Littlefield.

Hempel, C. (1965). "The Function of General Laws in History." In C. Hempel, ed., *Aspects of Scientific Explanation.*, 35–48. New York: Free Press.

Hobart, R. (1934). "Free Will as Involving Determinism and Inconceivable without It." *Mind* [vol. 43], 1–27.

Honderich, T. (1988). *A Theory of Determinism* [vol. 1 and 2]. Oxford: Oxford University Press.

———. (1993). *How Free Are You?* Oxford: Oxford University Press.

Horgan, T. (1985). "Compatibilism and the Consequence Argument." *Philosophical Studies* [vol. 47], 339–56.

Horgan, T., and M. Timmons (1993). "New Wave Moral Realism Meets Moral Twin Earth." In Heil (1993), 116–33.

James, W. (1897). "The Will to Believe." In W. James, ed., *The Will to Believe and Other Essays in Popular Philosophy*, 1–31. New York: Longmans, Green & Co.

———. (1962). "The Dilemma of Determinism." In *Essays on Faith and Morals*, 145–83. New York: World Publishing Company.

Johnson-Laird, P. N., and P. C. Wason. (1977). *Thinking: Readings in Cognitive Science*. Cambridge: Cambridge University Press.

Johnston, M. (1989). "Fission and the Facts." In J. Tomberlin, ed., *Philosophy of Mind and Action Theory*, 369–97. Philosophical Perspectives [vol. 3]. Atascadero, CA: Ridgeview.

Jones, W. T. (1992). "Deconstructing Derrida: Below the Surface of *Differance*." *Metaphilosophy* [vol. 23], 230–50.

Kahane, H. (1983). *Thinking about Basic Beliefs*. Belmont, CA: Wadsworth.

Kane, R. (1985). *Free Will and Values*. Albany: SUNY Press.

———. (1988). "Libertarianism and Rationality Revisited." *The Southern Journal of Philosophy* [vol. 26], 441–60.

———. (1989). "Two Kinds of Incompatibilism." *Philosophy and Phenomenological Research* [vol. 69], 219–54.

———. (1990). "Free Will Ultimacy, and Sufficient Reason." Paper read at the meeting of the American Philosophical Association, December, Boston.

———. (1993). "The Ends of Metaphysics." *International Philosophical Quarterly* [vol. 33], 413–28.

———. (1994A). "Free Will: The Illusive Ideal." *Philosophical Studies* [vol. 75], 25–60.

———. (1994B). *Through the Moral Maze: Searching for Absolute Values in a Pluralistic World*. New York: Paragon House.

———. (1996). *The Significance of Free Will*. New York: Oxford University Press.

Kant, I. (1965). *Critique of Pure Reason*. Trans. N. K. Smith. New York: St. Martin's Press.

Klein, M. (1990). *Determinism, Blameworthiness, and Deprivation*. Oxford: Oxford University Press.

Kuhn, T. (1962). *The Structure of Scientific Revolutions*. Chicago: University of Chicago Press.

Lewis, D. (1973). *Counterfactuals*. Cambridge: Harvard University Press.

———. (1981). "Are We Free to Break the Laws?" *Theoria* [vol. 3], 113–21.

———. (1993). "Causal Explanation." In Ruben (1993), 192–206.

Lipton, P. (1991). *Inference to the Best Explanation*. London: Routledge.

Lucas, J. R. (1993). *Responsibility*. Oxford: Clarendon Press.

Mackie, J. L. (1977). *Ethics: Inventing Right and Wrong*. New York: Penguin Books.

———. (1982). *The Miracle of Theism*. Oxford: Oxford University Press.

Magill, K. (forthcoming). *Freedom and Experience*.

Mele, A. (1995). *Autonomous Agents*. New York: Oxford University Press.

McCall, S. (1984). "Freedom Defined as the Power to Decide." *American Philosophical Quarterly* [vol. 21], 329–38.

Moore, G. E. (1968). *Principia Ethica*. Cambridge: Cambridge University Press.

Morse, S. (1994). "Culpability and Control." *University of Pennsylvania Law Review* [vol. 142], 1587–1660.

Nagel, T. (1979). *Mortal Questions*. New York: Oxford University Press.

———. (1986). *The View from Nowhere*. New York: Oxford University Press.

Nathan, N. M. L. (1992). *Will and World*. Oxford: Oxford University Press.

Nisbett, R., and L. Ross (1980). *Human Inference: Strategies and Shortcomings of Social Judgment*. Englewood Cliffs, NJ: Prentice-Hall.

Nisbett, R., and T. Wilson (1977). "Telling More Than We Can Know: Verbal Reports on Mental Processes." *Psychological Review* [vol. 84], 231–59.

Nozick, R. (1981). *Philosophical Explanations*. Cambridge: Harvard University Press.

O'Connor, T. (1993). "Indeterminism and Free Agency: Three Recent Views." *Philosophy and Phenomenological Research* [vol. 53], 499–526.

———. (1995A). "Agent Causation." In O'Connor (1995B), 173–200.

———., ed. (1995B). *Agents, Causes, and Events*. New York: Oxford University Press.

Popper, K. (1965). "Of Clocks and Clouds." Arthur Holly Compton Memorial Lecture. St. Louis: Washington University.

Puccetti, R. (1981). "The Case for Mental Duality." *The Behavioral and Brain Sciences* [vol. 4], 93–123.

Putnam, H. (1962). "It Ain't Necessarily So." *The Journal of Philosophy* [vol. 59], 658–71.

———. (1987). *The Many Faces of Realism*. Lasalle, IL: Open Court.

————. (1992). *Renewing Philosophy*. Cambridge: Harvard University Press.

Quine, W. V. O. (1960). *Word and Object*. Cambridge: MIT Press.

Ravizza, M. (1994). "Semi-Compatibilism and the Transfer of Non-Responsibility." *Philosophical Studies* [vol. 75], 61–93.

Rawls, J. (1971). *A Theory of Justice*. Cambridge: Harvard University Press.

Rorty, R. (1979). *Philosophy and the Mirror of Nature*. Princeton: Princeton University Press.

————. (1982). *Consequences of Pragmatism*. Minneapolis: University of Minnesota Press.

————. (1989). *Contingency, Irony, and Solidarity*. Cambridge: Cambridge University Press.

————. (1993). "Putnam and the Relativist Menace." *The Journal of Philosophy* [vol. 90], 443–61.

Ruben, D., ed. (1993). *Explanation*. Oxford: Oxford University Press.

Russell, B. (1925). *What I Believe*. New York: Dutton.

————. (1966). "Pragmatism" and "William James's Conception of Truth." In Russell, *Philosophical Essays*, 79–111, 112–30. New York: Simon and Schuster.

Sartre, J. (1956). *Being and Nothingness*. New York: Philosophical Library.

Sayre-McCord, G., ed. (1988). *Essays on Moral Realism*. Ithaca: Cornell University Press.

Schlick, M. (1939). *Problems of Ethics*. New York: Dover.

Schoeman, F., ed. (1987). *Responsibility, Character, and the Emotions*. Cambridge: Cambridge University Press.

Searle, J. (1969). *Speech Acts*. Cambridge: Cambridge University Press.

————. (1983). *Intentionality*. Cambridge: Cambridge University Press.

Sellars, W. (1963). *Science, Perception and Reality*. New York: Humanities Press.

Singer, I. (1993). "Freedom and Revision." Paper read at the meeting of the Pacific Division of the American Philosophical Association, March, San Francisco.

Skinner, B. F. (1971). *Beyond Freedom and Dignity*. New York: Knopf.

Skinner, E. (1995). *Perceived Control, Motivation, and Coping*. Thousand Oaks, CA: Sage Publications.

Slote, M. (1982). "Selective Necessity and the Free Will Problem." *The Journal of Philosophy* [vol. 79], 5–24.

Smart, J. J. C., and B. Williams, eds. (1973). *Utilitarianism: For and Against*. Cambridge: Cambridge University Press.

Smilansky, S. (1994). "The Ethical Advantages of Hard Determinism." *Philosophy and Phenomenological Research* [vol. 54], 355–63.

Smith, E., and D. Medine (1981). *Categories and Concepts*. Cambridge: Harvard University Press.

Sorell, T. (1994). *Scientism*. New York: Routledge.

Stich, S. (1990). *The Fragmentation of Reason*. Cambridge: MIT Press.

Strawson, G. (1986). *Freedom and Belief*. Oxford: Oxford University Press.

———. (1994). "The Impossibility of Moral Responsibility." *Philosophical Studies* [vol. 75], 5–24.

Strawson, P. (1962). "Freedom and Resentment." In Watson (1982), 59–80.

———. (1980). "Reply to Ayer and Bennett." In Van Straaten (1980), 260–68.

Taylor, R. (1966). *Action and Purpose*. Englewood Cliffs, NJ: Prentice-Hall.

———. (1974). Metaphysics. 2d ed. Englewood Cliffs, NJ: Prentice-Hall.

Tomberlin, J., ed. (1989). *Philosophical Perspectives* [vol. 3]. Atascadero, CA: Ridgeview.

Unger, P. (1984). *Philosophical Relativity*. Minneapolis: University of Minnesota Press.

———. (1986). "The Cone Model of Knowledge." *Philosophical Topics* [vol. 14], 125–78.

———. (1995). "Contextual Analysis in Ethics and Epistemology." *Philosophy and Phenomenological Research* [vol. 55], 1–26.

van Inwagen, P. (1974). "A Formal Approach to the Problem of Free Will and Determinism." *Theoria* [vol. 40], 9–22.

———. (1975). "The Incompatibility of Free Will and Determinism." *Philosophical Studies* [vol. 27], 185–99.

———. (1980). "The Incompatibility of Responsibility and Determinism." In M. Bradie and M. Brand, eds., *Action and Responsibility*, 30–37. Bowling Green, OH: Bowling Green State University.

———. (1983). *An Essay on Free Will*. Oxford: Oxford University Press.

———. (1989). "When Is the Will Free?" In Tomberlin (1989), 399–422.

Van Straaten, Z., ed. (1980). *Philosophical Subjects: Essays Presented to P. F. Strawson*. Oxford: Oxford University Press.

Waller, B. (1990). *Freedom Without Responsibility*. Philadelphia: Temple University Press.

Watson, G. (1975). "Free Agency." In Watson (1982), 96–110.

Watson, G., ed. (1982). *Free Will*. New York: Oxford University Press.

Watson, G. (1987). "Responsibility and the Limits of Evil: Variations on a Strawsonian Theme." In Schoeman (1987), 256–86.

Williams, B. (1973). *Problems of the Self*. Cambridge: Cambridge University Press.

———. (1981). *Moral Luck*. Cambridge: Cambridge University Press.

Wolf, S. (1990). *Freedom within Reason*. New York: Oxford University Press.

Zimbardo, P., and M. Leippe (1991). *The Psychology of Attitude Change and Social Influence*. New York: McGraw-Hill.

Index

appeal to fear, 136
appeal to glory, 135
Aristotle, 45, 86, 90–91, 134, 164
armchair social science, 53–54, 119, 162–63
Armstrong, D., 44
Augustine, 21
Austin, J. L., 27, 28, 94, 96, 157
autonomy, 116
Ayer, A. J., 13, 27, 69, 91, 100, 130, 137, 144, 145, 150, 153–54

baldness example, 111, 114–19
Baudelaire, C., 24
belief-relativism, 7
Bennett, J., 64–65
Berkeley, G., 32, 43, 91
Bernstein, M., 34, 47, 110, 111, 113, 162
Blackburn, S., 126
Blumenfeld, D., 85
Boyd, R., 6, 36
Brink, D., 26, 36
Brook, R., 111

Cambridge changes, 92
Campbell, C. A., 46, 58
Campbell, J., and R. Pargetter, 36
Camus, A., 24, 25, 43, 76
Castañeda, H. N., 154
Chisholm, R., 62, 157
Clarke, R., 10, 46, 58, 62, 69, 72–74, 75
Clifford, W. K., 36, 54
Cockburn, D., 62, 109–10, 112, 115, 119–21

compatibilism, 63, 69, 79, 82, 86, 88–89, 101–3, 115–17, 119, 122, 130, 131, 136–37, 138–39, 141, 151, 160–61
compensatory justice, 157
Comte, A., 24
Confucius, 162
consequence argument, 82–86, 102, 106
Cornman, J., 33

Darwin, C., 24
deconstructionism, 46
Dennett, D., 10, 26, 62, 66, 81, 82, 95, 100, 101, 108, 136, 137
Descartes, R., 21, 89, 135
desires-for-philosophy, 4, 19, 22, 33–36, 156, 159
determinism, 6, 58–59, 83–86, 139
Dewey, J., 24, 25, 38
Dostoevski, F., 160
Double, R., 3, 13, 31, 38, 45, 57, 66, 72, 85, 107, 112, 120, 122, 126, 139
Drey, W., 46
dualism, 160

Einstein, A., 18
entailment, 146–47
epistemological skepticism, 8, 26, 32, 41–43, 49, 50–51, 88–89
explanation, 42, 45–46, 69–76, 91, 124

fact-value distinction, 5, 46–57, 141, 155, 161
fatalism, 136

Feuer, L., 25
Feuerbach, L., 25
Feyerabend, P., 42
Fichte, J., 32
Fischer, J., 9, 83, 144, 157
Flew, A., 61, 100
fragmentation problem, 61, 111–21
Frankena, W., 144
Frankfurt, H., 10, 77, 82, 86–90, 130, 137, 157
free choice defined, 10–12
free will and the law, 28–29
free will defense, 128
free-will-either-way theory, 102–3, 123, 141, 160–61
free will exemplars, 107
free will subjectivism, 3–4, 10, 12, 13, 78–82, 96, 159–61
freeness facts, 141
French, P., 77, 94–96
Freud, S., 24

Galileo, 18
Ginet, C., 46
Glover, J., 144
Goethe, W., 24
Goldman, A., 53
Gore, A., 106

hard determinism, 13, 79, 82, 140, 159–60
Harman, G., 44, 45, 91, 126, 127, 132–34
Heartless Beings, 66
Hempel, C., 45, 46, 76
Hobart, R., 69, 130, 137
Hobbes, T., 10, 86, 100
Honderich, T., 10, 13, 28, 45, 50, 115, 136
Horgan, T., 83
Horgan, T., and M. Timmons, 36, 44
Hume, D., 13, 20, 32, 46–47, 48, 49, 78, 86, 91, 100, 101, 143–55, 165

incompatibilism, 79, 82–86, 89, 101–3, 115–16, 119, 122, 131, 141, 151
indexical terms, 114
inference to the best explanation, 21, 50
intermediate-level principles, 33, 40–55, 100, 141, 155, 156
introspection, 42

James, W., 19, 25, 32, 36, 38, 73, 136
jerks, 105–6, 113–14
Johnson-Laird, P. N., and P. C. Wason, 21
Johnston, M., 43
Jones, W. T., 46

Kahane, H., 59–60
Kane, R., 6, 10, 24, 35, 43, 62, 69–72, 79, 82, 101, 117, 134–36, 139, 160
Kant, I., 20, 21, 24, 25, 31, 32, 44, 52, 104, 135
Kapitan, T., 127
Kierkegaard, S., 24
Klein, M., 127, 134–35
Kuhn, T., 82

Larkin, P., 135–36
Lehrer, K., 157
Lewis, D., 27, 72
libertarianism, 10, 69–76, 79, 82, 117, 130, 131, 134–36, 160
Lipton, P., 29, 74, 83
Loch Ness monster, 69
Locke, J., 86
logical positivism, 27, 44, 100
lower-level theories, 3, 33, 49–53
Lucas, J. R., 31–32, 77, 91–93, 136

Mach, E., 19
Mackie, J. L., 36, 44, 45, 91, 126, 144, 145, 150, 153, 162

Magill, K., 11, 129
magnanimity, 138–41
Marx, K., 21, 24, 25
materialism, 160
McCall, S., 139
Mele, A., 45, 103, 110, 122–24, 145
metaphilosophy, 3, 8–9, 22–32, 33, 49–53, 141, 156, 163–64
metaphysical realism, 6–7, 43–44, 113
Milesian philosophers, 21
Mill, J. S., 78, 86
Milton, J., 24
Moore, G. E., 27, 60, 88, 127, 130, 131, 157
moral argument for the existence of God, 120–21
moral realism, 65, 67–68, 78–82, 144, 160–61, 162, 163
moral responsibility, 11–12, 58–60, 63–69, 74, 82–86, 91–96, 103, 119, 144–46, 164
moral responsibility defined, 145
Morse, S., 28–29
murderous demon example, 74–75

Nagel, T., 13, 29, 45–46, 59, 73, 75, 77, 91, 93
Nathan, N. M. L., 135
Neurath's boat, 114
Newton, I., 24
Nietzsche, F., 21, 24, 163
Nisbett, R., and T. Wilson, 42
no-free-will-either-way theory, 102–3, 123, 141, 160
normal philosophy, 82, 87–88
Nozick, R., 6, 29 ·

Occam, W., 44, 45
O'Connor, T., 62, 69
ontological conservativism, 44–45
open-question argument, 66, 127, 130–32

ordinary language philosophy, 21, 27–28
Original Sin, 157

phenomenology, 21
Philosophy as Continuous with Science, 30–32, 50–51, 53–55, 96, 99, 101, 104, 110–11, 114, 119, 120–21, 125, 126, 141, 163–64, 165
Philosophy as Conversation, 24–25, 76, 81–82, 89, 93, 96
Philosophy as Non-Continuous with Science, 31, 52–53, 119, 121, 157
Philosophy as Praxis, 24, 25–26, 50, 52, 60, 62, 68, 76, 80, 86, 93, 96, 100, 110, 121, 124, 157
Philosophy as Underpinnings, 26–29, 60, 62, 68, 76, 80–81, 86, 90, 96, 100, 110, 121, 124, 157
Philosophy as Worldview Construction, 29–32, 50, 68–69, 80, 84, 90, 93, 95, 100, 159, 165
Plato, 18, 20, 24, 25, 47, 52, 63, 65, 67, 92, 105, 110–11, 162
Popper, K., 136
postmodernists, 5, 22
principle of alternative possibilities, 86–90
principle of rational explanation, 72
Puccetti, R., 117–18
Putnam, H., 8, 25, 37, 45, 137
Pythagoras, 24

quantum indeterminacy, 70–71, 139
Quayle, D., 106
Quine, W. V. O., 30, 42, 44, 45, 60–61, 91, 114

Ravizza, M., 87–88
Rawls, J., 9, 25–26
reflective equilibrium, 9, 33
Reid, T., 27

retribution, 124, 138
revolutionary philosophy, 82, 88
Rorty, R., 8, 22, 24, 32, 42, 50, 54,
    135–36, 157, 159, 162
rule of reciprocity, 90
Russell, B., 19, 36, 91, 139, 163

Sartre, J. P., 17, 24, 135, 163
Schlick, M., 65, 66, 69, 100, 130
Searle, J., 34, 127–28
Sellars, W., 30, 32, 42, 61, 91
Singer, I., 56–57
Skinner, B. F., 63
Skinner, E., 12
Slote, M., 83
Smart, J. J. C., 85
Smilansky, S., 114
Smith, E., and D. Medin, 115
soft determinism, 79, 82
Sorell, T., 30
Spinoza, B., 136
Stich, S., 43, 50, 53
Stoic philosophy, 53, 54, 164
Strawson, G., 13, 80, 82, 116, 135
Strawson, P., 10, 13, 60, 63–69, 81, 102

Taylor, R., 100
truth-tracking goals, 6, 7, 29, 32, 48,
    51, 54–55, 163–64

ultimate responsibility, 127, 130,
    134–38
Unger, P., 13, 88–89, 100
unity objection, 110–11
utilitarianism, 104

values subjectivism (moral non-
    realism), 5–6, 13, 34–36, 46–47,
    78–82, 108, 111, 130, 142, 144,
    149–50
Van Inwagen, P., 10, 58, 77, 82–86,
    89, 102, 106, 157
verificationism, 158–59

Waller, B., 11–12, 82, 144, 146
Watson, G., 64, 82
Williams, B., 126
Wittgenstein, L., 25, 42, 62, 110
Wolf, S., 56–57, 135, 152

Zimbardo, P., and M. Leippe, 90